THE WOMB IN WHICH I LAY

THE WOMB IN WHICH I LAY

Daughters Finding Their Mothers in Life
and in Death

Pauline Perry

Souvenir Press

Contents

Foreword   vii

Chapters
One.   The Unique Relationship   1
Two.   Is Love Enough?   13
Three.   Early Memories: Daddy's Girl   21
Four.   Early Memories: Mummy and Me   38
Five.   Work, Sex and Children: Adult Relationships   56
Six.   Time of Parting   76
Seven.   The Comfort of Ritual   94
Eight.   Grief and Guilt   112
Nine.   Loving in Finding   131
Ten.   Finding the Answers   143

References   161

Foreword

Writing about mothers and daughters is a daunting task. So many moving biographies and novels, and so many excellent personal accounts of the relationship have been written that it is difficult to select from such a wealth of resource. The hardest task, though, is to remain objective about the experience of other women and the wisdom of many experts when the topic is one so very personal.

I have tried in writing about daughters' stories of their mothers' loss not to intrude my own experience too often or in too much detail. Nevertheless, thoughts of my own mother and my own struggle to come to terms with the emotions surrounding her death have never been far from my thoughts as I wrote. In a very real sense, this book is my tribute to her. Indeed, the inspiration for this book came from my experience of losing her, and the many conversations I had with other women who shared their feelings and thoughts about their own mothers at that time.

I am also the mother of three sons and a daughter. Inevitably, then, two thoughts have been constantly in my mind. First, I have been conscious that in the course of things my beloved daughter may one day evaluate our relationship when I am no longer here, just as the women of whom I have written in this book have done. That is an awesome thought! I hope she will find it in her generous heart to forgive the things I got wrong, and that the doubts some women feel as to whether they were truly loved by their mother will never plague her. There certainly is not one single incident for which she should suffer guilt.

Secondly, in writing about the unique relationship of mother and daughter, I would not for a moment wish to undervalue or down-play the importance of the mother-son relationship. My adored sons have been a source of unalloyed joy for me from the moment of their births, and I firmly believe that they know that well. As one who has been further blessed with a dear husband who has been the best of fathers to our sons and our daughter, I am also most happily aware of the centrality of those relationships in all their lives. Because this book is not about those relationships does not imply that they are less precious or worthy of study.

The ten women who were interviewed for this book gave generously of their time, and even more generously of their innermost feelings in talking to me. Most of all, I owe to each of them a huge debt. They *are* the book – without them it could not have been written. Although they are all in different ways quite remarkable women, their stories, their grieving and their 'finding' are, I believe, stories which speak to any woman who loses a mother. I only hope I have been able to do justice to them and to their honesty and openness in what I have written here.

I had no idea, when I embarked on this project, just how widely it would be possible to roam through the literature of the social scientists, philosophers and theologians for material which threw light on the experience of bereavement and the relationship of mothers and daughters. I have learned much, and have tried to pass on some of what I have learned. Again, I hope that in so doing I have done justice to the richness of the academic fields through which I have wandered.

I owe a special debt to the poet Wanda Barford, whose poems to her mother moved me deeply when I first read them, and later when I heard her read from them at a conference of the Council for Christians and Jews. To her and her publishers, Flambard Press, I am grateful for permission to reproduce some of her lovely words.

My personal and heartfelt thanks are due to Souvenir Press and to the great and inspiring personality of its Managing Director, Ernest Hecht. His encouragement, helpfulness and faith in the topic has kept me going and given me a real enjoyment of the work throughout.

Foreword

If in writing this book I have offered some food for reflection, thought and comfort to daughters who are grieving for their mothers, then I shall be well content.

Pauline Perry
London, November 2002

Chapter One
The Unique Relationship

I was a grown-up, middle-aged woman of fifty when my mother died. I had a happy marriage, a fulfilling career, and four much loved and loving children. It should have been possible to accept her death at the age of eighty-eight as a sad but natural part of the cycle of generations. But no, it wasn't like that: the day my mother died is etched in my mind as a dark day of unbelievable and mind-numbing grief of a nature I had never experienced before. I felt quite literally and totally bereft, an orphan, crying for comfort which only my mother could give. For months afterwards I would actually look forward to the moment of getting back from work, where I had to act as if nothing was wrong, so that I could retreat to my bedroom and weep like the lost child I felt I had become.

Ours was no easy relationship. Like all too many women of my generation, I had seen in my childhood a mother of formidable talent and intellect frustrated and angry at her role of 'housewife', a shadow to her husband's career. After she died I felt enormous guilt that for much of our lives I had treated her with something akin to contempt because of her lifestyle. Only then, when it was too late, did I begin to understand her, and feel both heart-aching sympathy for the waste of her talent, and gratitude for the life of sacrifice she had lived to ensure that her daughters had opportunities to break from the mould which confined her. 'If only' I now say 'I had been able to say this to her while she was here'. Speaking to the women whose stories are told in this book, I realise that 'if only' is a common theme of daughters as they

1

acknowledge, often after their mother's death, all that she was for them.

The bond of mother to daughter seems to be universal, no matter how different the circumstances and cultures. I was moved to hear First Lady Laura Bush, asked in an interview a day or two after the fateful date of 11 September 2001, what she thought and did on her extraordinary journey to the Presidential secret hideout. She replied that after speaking to her daughters to make sure they were safe, she had called her mother. 'Why did you do that?' asked the interviewer. The First Lady thought for a moment. 'For the comfort of her voice,' she replied.

In those simple words, Laura Bush expressed the reality of the eternal bond of women across generations – mother to daughter to mother. When the world outside feels suddenly threatening and we are fearful, the toughest daughter may turn to her mother for comfort, just as she did as a little girl long ago. The mother who nurtures and protects is also the daughter who turns to her own mother for the comfort she has learned throughout life to expect from her mother's presence, from the sound of her voice. September 11 may have been the day the world changed in many ways, but the relationship between mother and daughter was unchanged and strong for the First Lady, and for many thousands of other troubled, anxious and bereaved women on that as on many another sad day.

Mothers and daughters fight, laugh, collude and compete, wound and heal, exclude and share, over and over again, but the relationship is unique and inescapable. Love her or hate her, respect or reject her, admire or revile her, your mother is the model of womanhood you first experienced, the woman whose role in the family and in society you first observed, the giver of life and care from your first breath, the transmitter of the genes you carry through life, the womb in which you lay.

We shall hear women tell the story, in their own words, of their relationships with their mothers, their lives together and apart. They tell us of their childhood memories of their mother; their adult relationship; and the influence these have had on their ways of dealing with their own lives. They speak also of how they faced the final parting, when the death of their mother brought at first intense and unbelievable pain, but later new and healing understandings. Death brought one stage of the relationship to an end, but each learned in different ways that the lifelong dialogue between our mothers and ourselves transcends their death.

The ten women I interviewed told me about their experience of the loss, the moment of parting, and the period of intense emotions before and after their mother's death. They spoke of their painful and conflicting emotions as they dealt with the arrangements for cremations and burials, and the sadness of sorting out their mother's possessions, often full of mementoes from their own long-buried past. Listening to their stories, I also heard how they have managed to move on with the rest of their lives – sometimes unexpectedly strengthened by learning truths about themselves and about their mothers. In different ways, each woman has spent long years in finding their mothers as adult women, and seeing their mothers after death in a new and clearer light.

Many speak of the presence of their mothers, felt long after death, at key moments in their lives. One prominent woman financier once told me, 'Sometimes when I feel things going wrong in a Board meeting, and I feel near to panic, I just imagine she's with me, and suddenly I am strong again'. Another said, 'Whenever I go into an intimidating environment, like a meeting with a Secretary of State, or a member of the Royal family, I just pause outside for a moment, and I wrap the cloak of my mother around me. Then I am strong.'

Less happily, another woman of the same generation, tortured by uncertainty over her mother's love for her, said, 'Although it's years since she died, when people are talking about quite different matters, suddenly something triggers thoughts of my mother, and instantly her hugeness fills the room for me. My day is clouded by my dark thoughts. I shall never know now whether she really loved me.'

The women whose stories are told here are, as it happens, successful and often prominent women in their own field. Some came from very modest backgrounds, and many of their mothers' lives were lives of educational, social and financial deprivation, as well as of the poverty of opportunity that was the almost universal lot of their generation. Some were the daughters of very happy marriages; others were the daughters of a single parent. Some saw the model of a working mother, others the example of a full-time mother at home absorbed in domestic cares. What became very clear as they spoke was that even though their mothers may have been restricted in career opportunities, the remarkable women to whom I spoke are the daughters of remarkable mothers.

Common themes in their stories are how their mothers wanted 'the best' for these daughters, and how, despite the difficulties of their generation of women, they often gave to their daughters examples of excellence in the skills and activities they were able to pursue. Despite the ups and downs of many mother-daughter relationships described, the one inescapable truth of all the stories is the overwhelming importance of mothers to their daughters: the sense of a lifetime dialogue between them, which even death does nothing to silence. One noted opera singer once said to me, 'When I am given awards and honours, I still say to my long-dead mother, ''There you are, Mother, is that enough?'' I still long for the approval I never felt sure she gave when she was alive.'

Although their mothers were not well known in the world outside the family the stories their daughters have to tell show how much they derived from their mothers. Their mothers played an often unrecognised part in building and fuelling the fire and spirit which turned their daughters into confident and successful women, many of them quite outstanding high achievers.

Parents and children, regardless of gender, form their own, special and deep relationships. Fathers and daughters have a love and delight in each other which is legendary; mothers and sons love each other fiercely and with a strength of attachment which has become the material for many a tale in both serious and popular literature: fathers and sons have their own movingly deep relationship, providing often inspiration and model for male behaviour across the generations. Much has been written about all these relationships. This book is about mothers and daughters.

The relationship between mother and daughter, as psychologists and other social scientists recognise, is one which is more enduring through life, the boundaries between the two people more fluid, than in any other relationship in the family. All but an unlucky few children, boys and girls, begin life in the intense and close relationship – the love affair as some have called it –

between mother and baby that follows from the birth of a baby throughout the early years. A son, though, will of necessity have to look to a male model, probably his father, to find his identity as he grows up, while a daughter will continue to identify in relation to her mother. Even if that identity is negative, defined as a determination to be as different as possible, as is common in the teenage years, nevertheless, the mother is still a key reference point in the daughter's search for who she is and will be, 'when I grow up'.

In her book *Altered Loves*, the Cambridge psychologist Dr Terri Apter, examines the relationship between adolescent daughters and their mothers. She comments that many early feminist psychologists saw this closeness as a weakness for women. Tied to their mothers' identity, which was so often one of under-achievement, they failed, so it was claimed, to find a firm direction for their lives, and so experienced that lack of self-confidence which prevented many young women in the 1960s and 1970s from achieving the success their intelligence, talent and education entitled them to expect. Others however see it as a strength, a rooting in confidence and in the female identity, which has enabled so many women to work together for their common goals.

Hope Adelman, who has written extensively and sensitively on the relationships of mother to daughter across many generations, says passionately that the bonds of mother to daughter are 'primal, immutable, revered'. She also has the insight to see that mothering a daughter is a tremendous challenge. Most of us would admit that it is a challenge to find the right balance between fostering the natural (and rewarding!) way in which our daughters identify with us as they grow up, and stepping back and allowing them to develop a separate identity. As a daughter struggles to become first a separate adolescent and then a self-confident adult woman, her success is largely determined by her mother's willingness to cooperate, and to let go at times and in areas where it is appropriate to 'stand back'.

Perhaps no generation of women has had to struggle with so huge a gap between their own lifestyle and that of their mother as those of us born in the middle decades of the twentieth century, when the world of our parents was grappling with the shadows of the Second World War. Young adults in an era when feminism was emerging, we were, willingly or unwillingly, wittingly or unwittingly, influenced by the debate about the role of women which burst into public consciousness during the 1960s and 1970s. Whatever our personal reactions to the feminist movement, we had to confront it and its after-effects in our lives. We were the generation for whom the contraceptive pill brought the possibility of reliable control over pregnancy into our hands, while our mothers' lives and sexual relationships were controlled by the fear of unwanted pregnancy to a degree hard to explain to our daughters. While many of our generation won battles for equality in every aspect of life, we were nevertheless raised by mothers for whom opportunity was severely limited, and whose personal expectations and ambitions all too often had to be confined to family and housework.

Early feminist literature of writers like Betty Friedan and Marilyn French in the USA, and Germaine Greer in the United Kingdom, charts in painful detail the frustration and despair of many women of that earlier generation. Friedan, a sociologist writing in 1963 in her groundbreaking book *The Feminine Mystique*, describes the lives of most women in her generation as 'comfortable, empty, purposeless'. In interviews with hundreds of women across the United States, she found only one who claimed to be perfectly happy with her life as housewife and mother – but that one too admitted finally and wistfully that she couldn't forever fill her life by having baby after baby.

The Women's Room, Marilyn French's novel, gives a graphic and moving account of the turning point in the lives of her women characters in 1970s' America – from dutiful wives to militant feminists, prepared to work and fight if necessary to ensure that life was different for their daughters. Germaine Greer, in her hugely influential book *The Female Eunuch*, first published in 1970, gave voice to the anger of many women who felt themselves to be enslaved by marriage. However, she also argued that the unsatisfactory ordering of relationships between the sexes cheated men as much as women. Another British academic Hannah Gavron, writing in the early 1960s, gave to her book charting her survey of women graduates' lives the title *The Captive Wife*, by which she summed up the experience of women of spirit, taught by their education to be free in thought and action, but discovering in their post-university lives that they were chained by society (and their husbands' acceptance of social values) to menial, servile work as home-makers with a limited prospect of escape.

That deprived and frustrated generation, however, was the generation of mothers who raised the women in these stories. Somehow, against that background of social circumscription of women's role, the mothers of the women whose voices we hear in these true accounts, managed to raise daughters who soared ahead of their mothers' dreams, many becoming leaders in their chosen field, role models for the generations following in their footsteps. Whatever mistakes these mothers may have made along the way, and however others may have seen them, their daughters' lives must be seen as a testimonial to their spirit. By what they gave, they played a key part in starting a new era in women's lives. Their daughters, now in their fifties and sixties, were the generation which breached the bastions of male domination in almost all sectors of national life: in boardrooms, academic life, politics and the media. In reflecting, as we often must do, how far we have to go in the equality equation, we should never forget just how far we have come.

The role of motherhood, and the attitudes and expectations towards it, have radically changed between these generations. The mothers of the women I interviewed raised their families at a time when it was tantamount to social and religious heresy to admit to anything other than joy and delight in the role of mother. Popular stories and films, as well as much media advertising, depended on the portrayal of motherhood as the ultimate goal and pleasure of every woman, bringing total fulfilment.

Many women of our mothers' generation were afraid of the consequences of breaking out of the mould of motherhood that was laid down for them. The lack of any legal or financial security meant that, for the majority, marriage was the only sure way of holding on to their own and their children's safety and security. It was also, for the women of the early twentieth century, the only role in which they could exercise any power. Much as they longed to see their daughters break out of the chains in which they had been bound, they feared for their daughters' safety if they broke out into an uncertain and hostile world.

If this seems fanciful to the young women of today, they would do well to read the best-selling 1978 book *Fat is a Feminist Issue* by the psychotherapist Susie Orbach. Speaking of the dilemma which faced the mothers of that time (and some would say it is not always so different even today), Orbach argued that every mother recognises the need for her to help her daughter into the social role of womanhood. The problem for a loving mother is that the world into which she must help her daughter to fit is a world of unjust inequalities between men and women. Much as she loves her daughter, and wishes her to be strong and grow without hindrance, she must also try to hold her daughter back from any impulse towards becoming the powerful and independent being which her brothers are encouraged to become.

The inherent ambivalence of the mother's message is enlarged by the mother's own dilemma in helping her daughter to grow into an independent woman. Orbach feels that this task presents the mother with an extremely painful choice. If she encourages her daughter to be like her, then she is condemning her to the same limited and powerless life that she herself has had. If on the other hand she encourages her to be different, then her own life lacks all validation. She does and does not want her daughter to follow her example, hence her ambivalent message.

Orbach believed that this ambivalence was at the heart of mother-daughter relationships. The confused message of 'I love you, and I want you to be strong and self-fulfilled, but I love you and I don't want you to be too strong and self-fulfilled, in case that exposes you to danger and makes my own life valueless' is an unhappy message both to give and to receive. Our generation of mothers, by and large, accepted no such reservations about conveying only the positive message to our daughters. But we can never forget that we were ourselves recipients of the confused message, and deep within our psyche some of that ambivalence and self-doubt can still and painfully be found.

It took the writings of anthropologists like Sarah Hrdy to give an academic interpretation to the outburst of honesty about the mixed emotions of motherhood which had come from the feminists of the 1960s and 1970s. In her illuminating book *Mother Nature*, published in 2000, Professor Hrdy untangles the conflicting strands of motherhood. Ruthless and competitive but also tender and nurturing, the patterns which are and have been seen in the behaviour of our evolutionary animal ancestors across millions of years throw new light on the behaviour of human mothers.

Hrdy's view of motherhood is, as she herself describes it, evolutionary and comparative. She challenges the Darwinian view of women as passive reproducers, and observes that the female primates of her studies are in a real sense full participants in the fight for survival, just like their male counterparts. They make carefully balanced and highly informed choices about when to bear children and with what mates, how many children to have, and when to give attention to developing their own strength and weight rather than to their childbearing. Their love for their children is not incompatible with personal ambition, as for so long we women were taught. Indeed, in the world of primates observed by Hrdy and other comparative anthropologists, it becomes clear that ambition for one's own status and place in society is an essential ingredient in being a 'good' mother, since it is only in this way that the security and survival of one's children can be won. She also observes that there are bad mothers as well as good mothers – in primates as well as in the human species.

Hrdy's insight gives evolutionary meaning to Betty Friedan's assertion that ambition was not unfeminine and shameful. With breathtaking and (to her generation) shocking certainty, this feminist sociologist argued that it was ambition which made of a woman's life 'a work of art' and not just a series of 'haphazard incidents'. She was not of course advocating that all women should aspire to be running multi-national organisations or even rising to the top of their own career ladder. She was simply asking women to take control of their lives; to make the most of the talents they had been given, and to do their best for their families – ambitions which had always been applauded in their men folk.

The idea that it was not a disgrace for a woman to have personal ambition came as a stunning heresy to the generations of men (and women) who had assumed that women's role was as passive, submissive home-makers. Generations of writers, politicians and policy-makers had asserted that ambitious women were a danger both to society and to themselves.

Even after the First World War, when women had driven ambulances on to the fields of battle, and proved their courage and strength in difficult jobs at home, educated men in Cambridge University, for example, still argued that academic study and the competitive nature of academic life was unfeminine. Fortunately, by 1948 when women were at last admitted to membership of the University, these men were the minority. For fifty years before then, though, throughout the time when the mothers of the women interviewed for this book were growing up and seeking educational opportunities, their arguments had kept women out of full participation in the University's life. It has taken yet another generation to reach adulthood before the word 'ambitious' has lost its pejorative meaning, especially when used to describe a woman.

Small wonder then that during their adolescence, and sometimes for the whole of their mothers' lifetimes, some of the women interviewed for these stories rejected their mothers as role models, and chose at the conscious level to be like their fathers. In all too many cases, it is not until our mothers have died that we truly see them through an adult woman's eyes, and realise how, within the constraints of their society, they gave us examples on whose strength we have drawn through our own very different lives.

Only in the later and cooler-headed analysis of the past few years have we come to realise that the line between the career-minded woman and the full-time mother and housewife is not as firm as the popular wisdom of the 1970s and 1980s would have asserted. Women in different times and different cultures have had to learn to fight for their children's security in many different ways. In western societies, the mutual condemnation and open hostility between women who have made different life choices has been desperately unhelpful to the generation of mothers in the last half of the twentieth century. Many successful women will say that criticism from one's own sex for the choices, often painful, which have been made, is harder to bear than criticism from male colleagues or press pundits. It has also made honest and unbiased discussion of the issues very difficult indeed. Praising full-time mothers for their dedication brings storms of scorn and protest from working mothers, just as praise for women who are struggling to achieve some work-life balance between their jobs and family provokes outrage and condemnation from the mothers who stay at home.

Of one thing we can be sure, whatever the critics of older generations or conservative standpoints may wish to believe, and it is that millions of women around the world, by choice, balance exhausting and demanding jobs with joyful attention and care for their much loved children. Most of their children emerge intact, with a sense of their worth and the love that surrounds them. What I also know, and acknowledge with sisterly sympathy, is that for millions more there is no alternative to a combination of weary and back-breaking work with the care of children. Throughout the developing world, and amongst the poor of the developed countries, there simply is no luxury of choice. Yet the children of such mothers are loved and protected every bit as fiercely as the children of the wealthiest mother who is lucky enough to be able to choose to spend her time in full-time motherhood

The dispute between women about the proper role of mothers conceals of course the very real hurt, guilt and self-doubt that plagues so many western women of our generation. Recent research has shown that today's choices are still not easy. Sylvia Ann Hewlett's 2002 book *Baby Hunger* (published in the USA as *Creating a Life*) examines the desperate longing for motherhood experienced by many highly educated, high-earning women in the western world, and the frightening statistics of how many such women remain unwillingly childless. The price too many have paid for their career choices has been the inability to find the right partner or the right time to make motherhood possible – until at last they find their biology has caught up with them and it is too late.

The sociologists Arnot, Weiner and David, in their 1999 book *Closing the Gender Gap* examined how young women today speak about the choices they face in planning their adult lives. The researchers found that they use quite different language to describe their life choices from that used by their mothers and grandmothers. Where women who reached maturity in the first half of the twentieth century speak of doing 'what was expected' of them, or tell the researchers what they 'would have liked to do but it just wasn't possible' their daughters and grand-daughters say, 'I decided to . . .' The young women of today speak as individuals very much in control of their life choices, deciding freely the kind of woman they want to be.

Nevertheless what the young choose in this freedom is surprising. The authors of the report discovered that these 'free' choices are not the ones their feminist mothers expected them to make. Instead the majority of the young women interviewed at the end of the turbulent twentieth century reported choices which mirror the gender stereotypes of former generations. Not only are they clear that marriage and babies are a priority, but many are planning careers as hairdressers, secretaries, nurses and teachers: professions still traditionally dominated by women.

The first-wave feminists turned their backs on what they saw as sentimentality about motherhood. They wanted to be seen as cynical and tough and able to live their lives more like their fathers than their mothers. The young women of today – their daughters – are turning to a new mode of thought, accepting that the strength and power of emotion, emotional intelligence, and the capacity for 'sentiment' in the best sense of that word, are as important in business as in the family. Many are also happy to be sentimental about motherhood.

Chapter Two
Is Love Enough?

Literature is full of many wonderful examples which explore the mother-daughter relationship. Perhaps because it is so emotionally charged, and so central to women's lives, many such examples are written by authors about their own experience. This chapter tries to find the common themes which emerge in some of these examples.

In the following chapters, we meet the ten women I interviewed as daughters who had lost their mothers, and hear their story of their mother's lives, and their relationship with them. They were all fortunate in having mothers who were positive and loving to their children, although not all the relationships were easy, nor all the memories guilt-free. Many cried both bitter and grateful tears as they recalled all their mothers had meant to them as children. Many also wept, becoming lost little girls crying hopelessly for their mothers as they relived the days before and after their mother's death.

Not all mothers are such good examples; some daughters have to suffer negative and soul-destroying rejection and abuse from their mothers. The conflicting emotions such women feel as adults towards their mother was painfully expressed by one young woman who told me, 'I love my mother and I hate my mother; sometimes I feel my head will burst with trying to cope with both those feelings at the same time'.

Anne Robinson's *Memoirs of an Unfit Mother* describes her own confused feelings towards her difficult mother. This broadcaster and journalist comments that although we assume that of course we love our mothers, we are not told how to cope when our mother turns out to be unlovable. Robinson is now able to be both objective and forgiving about her own experience of mothering. She was raised by a mother she loved and who loved her, but that same mother, as an alcoholic, was unable to give her the care she needed. For the daughters of such inadequate mothers, learning how to separate our love and need of our mother from our anger at her bad behaviour can be one of the hardest parts of growing up.

The ten adult daughters speak revealingly of how it was after their mother's death. Often they have come to see their mothers in a completely new light. What they now see are the hidden strengths and determination within their mothers, which sadly some did not recognise until too late. One American woman, a senior academic, commented that as she was growing up, 'my mother was a joke: a silly housewife'. She was determined as a young girl to be as different from that as possible. 'I never really knew my mother until she died' she said, with painful tears running down her face, describing how, free of the need to maintain a separate identity from the living example of all she had rejected in her mother's lifestyle, she saw with clearer vision the strengths, the sadness, and the sacrifices, which had made up her mother's life. 'I wish so much I could tell her now how much I understand, and how sorry I feel for having belittled her life for all these years. I would so like now to be able to acknowledge my debt to her.'

Another woman spoke of her painful regret that she had never had the chance to talk to her mother about the understanding, which had only come after her death. 'I just wish I could have an hour with her now, to tell her how much I understand about her: how much I admire the strength it took to do all she did, even though it wasn't recognised in "career" terms.'

Just as for me in my grief and regret, the 'if only' theme appears in so many of the stories women tell about their feelings after the loss of their mother. Death clears the vision and removes the emotional clutter, so that we see our mothers as women in their own right, struggling, as we do, to do the best with the hand of cards life, and history, had dealt to them. A daughter's long and necessary battle for separate identity is sometimes ended only

14

in her mother's death. It is then that the futility and childishness of that battle becomes apparent, and we say 'if only . . .' If only we had shared our struggles with the one person who could have understood. If only we had given her the chance to tell us about her own painful life-choices, which turn out to have been not so fundamentally different from our own, if the different context is removed. If only we could tell her now how much we have come to understand; and if only we could say, woman to woman, daughter to mother 'Thank you'.

Of course, it is normal for adolescent daughters to try to throw off their identification with their mothers, whatever the circumstances of their lives. As the adolescent begins to shape her own identity, she must challenge her mother's beliefs, values and life-choices, even if at the end she adopts many of them as her own. The necessary process of determining oneself as a separate, individuated human being can sometimes lead to the pitched battles of adolescent daughters and mothers which are well documented in both folklore and experience.

The battles, however, are neither so fierce nor so all pervasive as some psychologists have described. The evidence from more recent studies shows that what has been called the 'April showers' of life – the adolescent period – is rather one of conflicting and varying emotions towards the mother figure as well as confusing changes in mood and behaviour. One moment the daughter will challenge her mother and fight with her fiercely over her choice of dress, friend, boyfriend or school subject, the next she will cling to her, seeking a return to the childhood experience of maternal nurture, closeness and care. Terri Apter has argued that this period of open conflict between mother and daughter is in reality only another manifestation of the deep bond between them. A daughter, she affirms, knows her mother's love is sure, and so knows that she can trust her mother, as probably no one else, 'with both her love and her rage'.

Terry Apter in her study of adolescent girls and their mothers (1990), found that in mid-adolescence the greatest need of the daughter from her mother is for validation of her dignity, an affirmation of her fragile sense of self and self-esteem. Apter describes the relationship in this period as 'asymmetrical emotional intimacy', by which she means that while the girls in her study wanted to be able to confide in their mother, tell her about their failures and triumphs, they did not want these confidences to be reciprocated. They shut out their mother's need to confide, to talk about her own feelings and experiences. In particular, the girls to whom she spoke disliked their mother trying to say 'I know how you feel'. The adolescent girl does not want to acknowledge too close an identity with her mother, and certainly does not want to know or recognise her mother's sexuality. This asymmetrical relationship can continue through life, with some adult daughters remaining needy for approval and applause in their success, or sympathy in their unhappiness, while rejecting even in later years their mother's need to benefit from the same intimacy and share her own anxieties or triumphs with the one woman she could best trust to hear them.

It was a hard and painful road of self-learning for me, as for many other women of middle age to find that the chance to listen to our mothers' confidences, to offer our understanding and comfort, has been lost for ever because of our failure to grow up. After our mothers are no longer here to tell us about themselves, we must set out to find them; to read the clues from letters and diaries, from the memories of others in whom they did confide, and from our own recollection of incidents of long ago, unclouded now by our more selfish needs.

The need to find one's mother, to know who and what she was, is most poignantly demonstrated by those who never knew their biological mother. Such examples are often told in literature and in biography. One fascinating example of the search for the 'real' mother comes in Margaret Forster's charming book *The Memory Box*. In this she tells the story of a young mother, Susannah, who had died when her daughter Catherine was a tiny baby. As an adult woman, Catherine finally opens the box of memories which her dying mother had so desperately put together almost thirty years earlier, as she prepared to leave behind her six-month-old baby. Catherine had no conscious memories of Susannah, and had attached herself completely to her stepmother. Indeed, for some years she had resisted opening the memory box, affecting no interest in it. After her stepmother's death, when she finally opens it the contents set her off on a long journey of discovery, to find who her mother was, and what she was trying to say in the messages that she had left for her beloved baby daughter.

What she found, as her young dying mother had fervently wished, was a real, vibrant and strong woman, far from the boring lifeless saint that her grandmother and even her father had portrayed. With amazement and delight, she found much of herself in her mother, and heard stories from long-ago friends and lovers that resonated with things she had never quite recognised or understood within her own personality. At the end of her long quest through the puzzles of the memory box, Catherine is free, as a woman, in a way she had never expected or dreamed. The gift her mother had given her, from the grave, was a new sense of self, and a new energy to get on with her life.

Another amazing example of the urgency of need to find the true mother, the womb in which we lay, is told in Campbell Armstrong's *All That Really Matters*. He tells the true story of his ex-wife's daughter, Barbara, who had been parted from her mother as a baby. Now over forty, and diagnosed with cancer, she determines to find her birth mother, even if only to see her once before she dies. She told her family that as she 'looked into the face of death', she was determined to set out in earnest on a search which she had first begun when she was a little girl of twelve. With their support, and after many unbearable frustrations, she finally succeeded in tracing her mother's brother. From him she learnt that her mother, Eileen, was living in the United States, but by an extraordinary coincidence, Eileen too was fighting cancer.

Eileen's brother was at first reluctant to allow Barbara to contact her mother, fearing that the shock would be too great for her in her failing health. Barbara had to wait several agonising months before at last Eileen was told that her daughter was trying to speak to her. Eileen was overwhelmed by the news, and moved to learn that her only daughter was still bearing the name she had given her when, as a single mother of only seventeen, and at her parents' adamant insistence, she had tearfully handed her over for adoption.

The reaction of both women to the news of the other's existence is recorded by Barbara's journal and by Campbell Armstrong's own memories. Eileen, tears running down her face, cried out repeatedly, 'Thank you God, thank you'. In the midst of her illness, suddenly there was the joy of finding her long-lost daughter. Even the news of Barbara's cancer could not dim her happiness and excitement. From Phoenix she phoned her daughter, far away in England. When she heard Barbara's voice on the other end of the line, she said simply 'This is your mother'.

Barbara later wrote in her journal that hearing those words gave her a feeling more intense than even the births of her own children. The pain which both had carried for long years, what Barbara had called the 'silent grief', was finally opened up and forgotten in shared tears, laughter and instant love.

Although the story is very different from the stories of the women in this book, it has strong parallels for all their stories, in that finding one's mother as a real woman – just like us – is one of the most important quests which we can pursue, since it is also a quest for our own identity. Sadly, for many, as indeed for me, this finding comes only after the death of our mother, and must be pieced together from scant clues and flashes of shared identity in unexpected events.

Many mother-daughter relationships contain elements of manipulation, competition, harsh judgement, rejection and displaced anger. This does not mean that the relationship is unimportant, either to the mother, whose own self-esteem and sense of identity is closely bound up with her daughter and their relationship, or to the daughter. The worst of mother-daughter relationships can still remain a determining feature throughout the daughter's life, influencing her choices and behaviour. No matter how we try, or how convincingly we deceive ourselves and those around us, most of us will find our identity has been hugely shaped by a struggle either to escape or to embrace the intimacy and identity which is the reality of our mother's womb in which we, the woman-to-be, once lay.

One of the most honest, even brutal, accounts of a mother and daughter of the generations we are considering comes in the brave 1987 memoir *Fierce Attachments* by Vivian Gornick. Vivian is a feminist and career woman; her mother's life was built around her marriage and family. Vivian and her Jewish mother are locked into a dialogue of hate and love. They walk endlessly around the streets of New York. Neither can leave the other alone, although the rage between them bubbles up with violence every so often, leaving both unhappy, with old wounds opened but never healed. They argue about Vivian's choice of men, just as fiercely as about the amount of coffee needed to make the right strength; about the mother's old stories of her childhood, and about the safety-pin in the hem of Vivian's dress. Yet they cannot stay apart.

The story is of a relationship too often seen between mother and daughter of those particular generations. Vivian longs for something – undefined – from her mother, while she also longs for the moment when she will feel free of her. Often they have long good times together remembering the tenement block in which they lived when Vivian was growing up, and the stories of the neighbours. The good times, though, never last. Locked together as each gets older, the mother turning eighty, they still walk and walk, and the repetition of their old stories, resentments and arguments goes on.

Vivian's mother needs and searches for her daughter's approval, but finds instead rejection of all that has been important in her life. She fights against her daughter's scorn by mocking all that Vivian achieves, vilifying her for her failed marriage, her political activities and the small and large successes which Vivian brings hoping for her approval. They cannot leave each other alone, because the mother needs reassurance from her daughter that her life was not meaningless, just as the daughter needs her mother to approve of her very different life-choices. Unresolved needs and unreal expectations tie them in unhappy bonds which prevent either from fulfilling their dreams and ambitions.

Near the end of her mother's life, Vivian tells of one stormy argument between them in her mother's apartment. Having said the most hurtful things they can find to each other, they sit together a long time in bitter silence. Vivian's mother breaks this silence at last by asking, with weariness rather than anger, why Vivian bothers to stay with her, why she doesn't simply walk away. 'I'm not stopping you,' she says. In a moment of bitter self-knowledge, Vivian sadly replies, 'I know you're not, Ma'.

What is clear is that even in the most unsatisfactory relationships, the need to find and understand our mothers cannot be escaped. Margaret Drabble, who has made public her antipathy towards her 'manipulative' mother, admits that her strange and often angry novel *The Peppered Moth* was written after her mother's death in an attempt to go 'down into the underworld' to try to find her. The book is the story – Drabble admits it is largely autobiographical – of a mother and daughter taking a cruise together, during which the mother dies. Drabble says in her afterword to the book, that this cruise was the one she should have offered to her mother, but did not. Although she can find scarcely a kind word with which to describe her mother, she also confesses that, since her mother's death, she thinks about her frequently. Quoting from an old Scottish ballad, she confesses; 'night and day on me she cries'.

Sometimes the understanding comes in the last years of our mother's life, as it did for the poet Wanda Barford, whose poems *A Moon at the Door* speak eloquently of a mother-daughter relationship which endured through the death of the mother. Speaking to her mother in one of their last times together, Wanda says

> What does it matter
> whether I like Karl Popper,
> whether you've read Auden on Kierkegaard
> or we both feel a rapport with Lautréamont?
> I love you. Isn't that enough?

Learning that the arguments and disagreements really don't matter, that it is enough just to know that there is love enough, is the most important point of resolution for both mother and daughter. Competition, yearning for recognition of each other's life styles, old bitterness and misunderstandings finally melt away, and each can say to the other, 'I love you. Isn't that enough?' and receive the answer 'Yes'.

Chapter Three
Early Memories: Daddy's Girl

As a little girl, I adored my father. He was indeed a wonderful, loving and joyous man, a huge personality who delighted in his daughters. I wanted to be identified with him, to be like him, because in my family he was the important achiever, and my mother was a nonentity – or so it seemed. Only now do I reflect that it was my mother who spent endless hours caring for me, alongside the considerable burden of running a household in wartime England. Only now do I recall the comfort of the feel of her when I sat on her knee to be cuddled and comforted according to my needs. Only now she is no longer here do I feel the overwhelming guilt that we would allow her to spend hours of every day cooking and clearing before and after meals while the rest of the family had important conversations with our father. That we were living out the gender stereotype of that generation is to me no comfort. She deserved better from us all.

Few little girls are either all Mummy's girl or all Daddy's girl, but the women described in this chapter felt themselves to have been 'Daddy's girl' in their early childhood, while those in the next chapter saw themselves as closer to their mothers in early childhood. Daddies and daughters often form a close, indeed adoring, relationship. Fathers famously delight in little girls to love and spoil, and for many little girls, Daddy is the hero against whom all men are judged even in adult life. Loving fathers can give their daughters a confidence in their ability to be loved by the opposite sex and can provide a window into the world of men. For my generation of women, Daddy also offered a model of the career-minded parent which our mothers were often unable to offer.

I was not the only girl who grew up with the example of a mother afforded the second-class status given to women of her generation – the generation born in or before the First World War (but, we should remember, the generation which also produced the crusading suffragettes who won votes for women). It was not surprising that we their daughters sometimes looked on their lives with dismay. Unable as young girls to see beyond the external quality of our mother's lives, many of us repudiated not the social mores which kept them as unpaid cooks and cleaners, but the women themselves. Their life, we said to ourselves, was not for us. How weak and foolish must our mothers be to put up with such a 'meaningless' life.

A moment's unclouded thought, of course, would have helped us to see the flaws in our perception. In the days of our childhood, there was a frighteningly limited choice for women. Marriage, and most of the mothers of women I interviewed for this book enjoyed a loving and satisfying marriage, was the most secure guarantee of financial and social security, as well as the only viable means of providing a home for themselves and their children to be together. As the anthropologist Sarah Hrdy would say, they, like their primate ancestors, were acting in the best way open to them to ensure their own and their children's security.

Few women in the first half of the twentieth century had private means, and married women had only restricted access to the funds needed for divorce proceedings or any hope of winning a settlement after divorce which would leave them with access to their children or financial support. If they found their lives literally intolerable, the stark choice was usually to give up their children and return to their parents or find work which for many would, in the absence of either experience or qualifications, be low-paid and as menial as the housework which had been their lot in marriage. Small wonder that most decided to stick it out, even in unsatisfactory marriages.

This model of women's lives, whatever the strains and frustrations it caused for individual women, worked tolerably well for society as it was until the middle of the last century. It began to break down as social and economic pressures changed the possibilities and expectations for women in later decades. The expansion of educational opportunity, the development of the contraceptive pill, the increased expectations of a standard of living which usually took two incomes to support, all made it necessary to re-think the old traditional roles. Carried forward and given an intellectual framework as well as an emotional passion by the feminist writers and thinkers of that time, the movement for change became unstoppable. Our mother's lives just would not work any more for most of the women of our generation. Something different had to be developed.

Children and teenage girls, however, rarely stop to consider the wider social issues. Many girls simply turned their backs on their mothers' lives and looked instead for a role model in what seemed to be the powerful figure of the family, their father. In so doing, they were not only rejecting their mothers' lives as they saw them, they were rejecting the received vision of what was 'feminine' and desired behaviour in women, compared to what were believed to be 'masculine' virtues and qualities which the women of the 1970s recognised as essential to their survival in the world in which they were then living.

Such flawed definitions of what is feminine or masculine have a long history. The feminist philosopher Dr Jean Grimshaw, in her 1986 book, *Philosophy and Feminist Thinking*, charts the way in which philosophy over the centuries has devalued those characteristics which are believed to be feminine. Aristotle believed that 'by nature' men were 'superior and ruler' while by their nature women were 'inferior and subject'. All most reassuring to those superior rulers, no doubt! More astonishingly, especially in the light of women's superior performance today in many of the linguistically related tasks of a modern economy, he believed that women were excluded from the full exercise of reason expressed in the faculty of speech, which he identified as the distinguishing human quality.

In the last century the existentialist philosopher and writer Jean-Paul Sartre (despite the living example of Simone de Beauvoir beside him to deny his prejudices) denigrates women as having minds incapable of the exercise which determines the human essence. He claims that while men's lives are occupied in 'filling empty places . . . establishing a plenitude', the 'obscenity of the female sex' is that everything about them, intellectually and emotionally, 'gapes open'.

De Beauvoir unfortunately seems to accept the logic of a fundamental difference between feminine and masculine qualities. In her best-selling book *The Second Sex* she argues not that these characteristics are complementary, necessary for human society in both men and women, but that girls should be raised and educated to be like boys; to acquire the same characteristics of fighting and dominating; experiencing what she calls 'subjective freedom' so that they can compete successfully in the new world which came into being after the Second World War.

It is that mistaken view, that women needed to become like men to survive, which dominated much feminist thinking in the 1960s and 1970s, while also sadly characterising the behaviour of a few of the women who first succeeded in scaling the heights of masculine enclaves in business and the professions. It also was this belief which determined the decision of 'Daddy's girls' in our generation to be like Daddy, and not like Mummy. We were reflecting reality as we saw it, and turning blindly from the evidence of the real strengths and riches of the 'feminine' characteristics which our mothers possessed, and which a sane world so desperately needs.

Although five of the ten women whose stories we follow describe themselves as being 'Daddy's Girl' while five others speak of a life locked in with their mother from the earliest days, all faced the challenge, as adults, of finding a role which was neither that which had served their mother nor that which had been filled by their father. Women of different generations are still searching for a way to achieve work-life balance; a way to contain within their lives their family ties, their career demands and their sexuality. The stories of the ten women I interviewed are reflections not only of their own experience, but of their generation. We shall hear their early memories of childhood, and meet their mothers in those memories. Later, we shall hear of their adult lives, and their mothers' part in those. To make it possible for them to speak freely about their memories and feelings, both sad and happy, the names they are given here are names of their own choosing but are not, in most cases, their own.

Judith

Judith, an elegant and highly intelligent blonde with a wicked sense of humour, is a successful businesswoman. In addition to building up a huge business from her family's firm, she became one of the United Kingdom's major authorities on retail business and has given generously of her time to many not-for-profit organisations, advising government departments and national bodies on such matters. She is an expert in many aspects of financial and retail business, and is a highly respected non-executive director of several major companies.

Judith always felt that she was 'Daddy's girl'. 'I didn't really like my mother when I was small,' she says. 'For me, my Daddy was perfect.' Judith's memories of her mother have become much clearer since her mother's death, however. 'I've grown to know my mother better since she died,' she now realises.

She has wonderful memories of her mother's happy, rejoicing spirit. 'I remember once when she came dancing into my bedroom, laughing and twirling around to show off the bright red cami-knickers my father had bought her. She was so full of life and joy.' Judith also recalls her mother's great entrepreneurial gifts. 'During the Second World War, recognising the commercial opportunities of property ownership, Mummy bought up retail property, even – somewhat to our alarm – selling her wedding ring and the family home in order to do so.' Although this seemed to her children a risky and inconvenient strategy, her shrewd business sense meant that she built up a profitable retail company that greatly enhanced the family's lifestyle.

Judith has no memory of her mother as a 'wife-at-home', in apron and slippers. Her mother, as she remembers her, was beautiful; always impeccably and fashionably dressed, with high heels and a great pride in her appearance. Judith was very conscious of the sexual electricity between her parents. Looking back, she feels that, for her at least, there was always competition for her father's attention. 'After your father has died, you can stop competing for his attention and you and your mother can get to know each other.' The incident with the red cami-knickers was significant both as evidence of a lively parental sexual relationship, and also as an example of their willingness to share the fun of that relationship with her.

Of particular significance to Judith was her mother's explanation of the family relationships. Perhaps because it summed up the exclusivity of the parental marital relationship, she is still uncomfortable with it today. Her mother said on more than one occasion, to Judith and her brother, 'Of course we love you, but you are a product of your father's and my love for each other, so that love must always come first.' To a young girl, that must have seemed a harsh thing to say – and yet, at the same time, something which made the preservation of marriage, and the family as a totality, of supreme importance. Her mother reinforced this by saying often, in words and in behaviour, 'Outside is the enemy. Only in the family are you safe.'

Judith respected and envied her mother's understanding of men. Born the last child of a family of thirteen, with lots of brothers, her mother had to jockey for her position in the family from an early age. She was known as a sickly child, despite her tremendous energy in adult life, but Judith felt that her mother's understanding of how to deal with men – and how to get her own way with them, in business or in social life – arose from this early family experience.

Judith's mother made all the family decisions. She was not only the business strategist; she also made all the key decisions about her children's schooling and friendships. When her and her husband's business success allowed them to make expensive choices for Judith and her brother, she it was who decided that Judith should attend one of the most exclusive and prestigious girls' schools in England. Judith recalls, 'She herself had minimum schooling, since her large family was not well off, and so the possibility of extended, never mind private, education was beyond their imagination. Nevertheless, she asked anyone whose opinion she respected what was the best girls' school in England. When she had received answers which agreed on a name, that was enough. She asked no further questions. If that was the best, then that was where I would go.' The fact that her daughter might find fitting into that rather rarefied environment less than easy did not seem to occur to her, and indeed Judith did fit in extremely well, after an intimidating start, and became both a popular and successful pupil of the school her mother had chosen for her.

Judith now acknowledges the importance of her mother's determination to give her 'the best' in everything. It is a realisation she cherishes, as proof of her mother's love for her, and she gladly pays tribute to the confidence and strength which that love and determination have given her.

Peggy

Peggy also describes herself as something of a Daddy's girl. She grew up thinking that her mother was 'not very bright'. 'My father was the clever one of the family, and it was him I always wanted to please. I felt she was always pleased whatever happened. I always saw her as a little housewife, and I knew I didn't want to be that.'

After leaving university, Peggy became a local government politician. She and her former husband shared a passion for politics from their university days. She rose through the ranks of one of our largest local authorities, to become Chair of its most influential committee. As part of her local government success, but more thanks to her immense administrative talent and strong personality, she has been active in the governance of several colleges and schools in her local area. She is a lively, attractive woman, with the pale reddish hair of her Celtic heritage, and a warm and affectionate personality.

Peggy's mother had grown up in a large family in the North East of England, with parents who were constantly on the move. Peggy's grandmother was a travelling cinematograph operator, and so left Peggy's mother to be brought up largely by her aunt. After her death, Peggy found a photograph of her grandmother in her mother's possessions, and under it, in her mother's handwriting, was the proud word 'Manageress'. When several younger siblings came along, Peggy's mother in her turn had to care for them. She left school at fourteen and went into apprenticeship as a tailor. Some of Peggy's best memories of her mother are of her exquisite tailoring and dressmaking. Peggy's father had started life in banking, but ran away with a friend of his, hoping to get to America. When he failed in that dream, he joined the army instead. He enjoyed wearing suits beautifully tailored by his wife. She even made her tiny daughter a little suit and cap from an RAF surplus blanket, which still features in early photographs.

Peggy remembers her parents' marriage as blissfully happy. 'They adored each other. They would work together on decorating the house they lived in – Mummy the expert, and Daddy holding the ladder for her or off to cook dinner while she perfectly matched rolls of wallpaper and paint. She loved the army life – most of all she loved the life of the sergeants' mess, and mourned it when Daddy was commissioned. She never enjoyed the officers' mess in the same way.' As a little girl, Peggy was clearly a rather special person to the troops on the camp. She remembers that she would sometimes be allowed into the sergeant's mess, and if she were lucky, she would be invited behind the big counter and given a rare chocolate bar. 'Once, before I started school at the age of three, I went out of the back gate in the garden on to the beach. There was a great panic, and half the army camp was out looking for me!'

Peggy remembers her mother as 'flirty, lively and very slim and attractive. She was happy – loved pretty dresses, parties and dancing, and longed to travel with her husband to some of the exotic places he was sent.' Such dreams were always curtailed by the need for her to stay and 'mind the children' for whom both parents were highly ambitious.

Her father was away much of the time during the Second World War, and Peggy with her sister and her mother moved back up to the North East to live with her maternal grandfather. Soon after they arrived, her grandfather had a stroke and her mother was much occupied in nursing him. Even this became impossible after a time, and he was taken into hospital. Peggy remembers 'going to visit him with Mummy in the nearby town. She would ride her bicycle, with me sitting on the handlebars, my feet in the big basket in front.' Later, her aunt, the wife of her father's brother, moved in as well, with her five children. For almost five years of Peggy's childhood, therefore, she lived in a house with seven children and two women in charge, the men of the family all distant – fighting a war, or ill in hospital.

After the war, the family moved into one of the 'pre-fab'

houses which appeared at this time all over the United Kingdom. Their happiness at being together again was marred for Peggy's mother by the arrival of her mother-in-law, who came to spend six months of every year with them. Peggy recalls her grandmother's unkindness to Peggy's mother. 'She made it clear that in her view her son had ''married beneath him'' and made no attempt to strike up any kind of friendly relations, even with her grand-daughters. After a few years of this, Mummy became ill – developing a rash over her entire body, even across her eyelids. Doctors diagnosed that she was suffering from extreme stress, and that finally made my father realise the strain she had been under.' His mother never came again to live with them.

In the post-war years, Peggy's mother was able to move out of her full-time role as housewife, and went to work in an expensive designer dress shop. Doing alterations of designer clothes she used her skills in a way which satisfied her. She was able to buy the clothes for her daughters at cut-price rates, and paid for them out of her wages. 'This', Peggy comments, 'was some consolation to us for coming home to a cold and empty house with Mummy not there. We really hated her being out at work.'

Peggy feels that she only really began to understand her mother after she had died. Many memories came back to her with new meaning at that time. 'I remember the day a plane came down in a nearby field during the war, and while everyone else was running away in panic, Mummy collected up scissors and ban-dages, and rushed out towards the burning plane to see if she could help the men inside. That took great courage.' Other mem-ories gave insight into her mother's great capacity for caring.

I also remember her compassion. When my little dog got distemper, Mummy couldn't bear to see her suffer. We had her put down, and then we buried her with ceremony in the garden. When my little sister got scarlet fever at the age of five, they took her off to hospital, and came and fumigated our bedroom. Mummy was very brave, for all our sakes, and went off on her bike every day to visit my sister in hospital. The only time she broke down and cried was when she saw that the hospital had washed my sister's pretty hair with carbolic.

It was not until Peggy was an adult, and when her politically active husband had just achieved an important post in his party, that her mother whispered in strict confidence that she was 'on their side' politically. This was the first time her mother demonstrated that she had a mind independent of Peggy's father, who was strongly opposed to his daughter's and son-in-law's brand of politics.

Such memories brought her mother into a new focus for Peggy. She realised how ambitious her mother had been for her, and how much her own strength, although used in different fields, mirrored strengths she had seen in her mother. 'She made me see that women can be independent and do things for themselves. She coped on her own when my father was away in the war. She managed the strain of running a big household in times that were hard both emotionally and financially. I owe to her the feeling that I can do difficult things – just as she tackled things that were supposed to be a man's work around the house.' Peggy also recognised that her mother's skill in tailoring and dressmaking, and 'her exquisite embroidery and crochet' were her generation's way of making the most of the available career opportunities. Although she had not appreciated these skills when she was a child, she now pays tribute to the excellence and hard work that went into the products she had taken for granted.

A.

A. was born in Bombay in India, into a close community of the Parsee religion. A. is so called because even in choosing a pseudonym for this book, she cannot, as a good Parsee, use a name that does not begin with the sacred letter assigned to her by the day and date of her birth. There are reasons for her caution. 'My mother wanted to call me "Sata" which is the word for "sweet", but I was quite a sickly baby, and she thought that maybe it was because she had used the wrong name. So she changed my name to one which began with A. as it was supposed to be.'

A. is herself a successful businesswoman, with a captivating

manner, and intelligent, beautiful eyes. She came to live in England after marrying an Englishman, and her energy and charm
have made her a popular member of the affluent community in
London where she lives.

A. was very close to her father.

I was very much 'Daddy's girl' when I was little. He and my
brother used to argue a lot, but he and I never did. My mother
told me that when I was born, he was very excited and said
to my mother, 'Mummy, Mummy, you've got a beautiful girl'.
He was a very gentle man.

He died when I was just fifteen, just as we had begun to be
friends as adults. For years I missed him.

A.'s mother and father were introduced to each other 'with a
view to marriage' by their parents. A explains:

It was not really an arranged marriage as we so often think of
such things, as a very free choice was offered to them by their
parents. They were allowed to go out together, and get to know
each other to see if they were suited. As it happened, they fell
very much in love, and were happily married and devoted
to each other until my father's untimely death at the age of
forty-five.

A.'s mother was the eldest of three children, the only girl and
very intelligent:

My mother was the brightest of the three. She was always top
of her class in school. When she was sixteen, she and her
mother travelled to Europe with her father. It was an exciting
trip, but she used to tell me how every day in the hotel she
was waiting to hear the results of her school-leaving examination. She should have been an engineer like her father, but
of course for a girl that was considered impossible. Her parents
did allow her to study for two years at college after school,
but then she got married. I remember her always with her nose
in a book, or listening to the BBC World Service, to keep up
with news and current affairs.

31

A.'s mother was not allowed to work or to follow a career, so she filled her time with charity work and sponsored many exhibitions of beautiful national handicrafts. A. recalls her mother's generous spirit. 'She couldn't do enough for her friends. Even when, on one occasion, one woman was unkind to her, she never said a word of criticism about that person, and when we grumbled about any of our friends, she would sit with us and try to help us see the other person's point of view.'

A.'s love of her mother is apparent in the way she remembers small but significant moments from her childhood.

> She had lovely eyes, and a lovely smile. I have such a strong memory of being with her on a train going to Ahmedebad when I was very little. I was sitting on her knee, and it was very hot. I can remember the feel of her sari – she wore such beautiful saris. She ordered a tray of tea to be brought to the compartment to cool us down. She would have liked more children, but my brother and I were born by caesarean section, and she was told not to have any more. I loved her very much, and I think she loved me. We did have 'spats' sometimes, but they never lasted long. I couldn't go to bed until she had said 'It's all right' and we were friends again.

Anne

Anne, a successful businesswoman and professional anthropologist, used to identify with her father when she was young, but remembers her mother as the strength of the family. 'It was no good arguing with her, because she used to make up her mind, and then that was right. She went with her feelings, and "the way the family lived" for her logic. To her, family were all the people she loved and who were close to her.'

Anne, with her dark eyes and hair, has a remarkably good academic and business brain, and has a strength which has taken her through some tough times in her own life. She is anxious to describe how beautiful her mother was. 'She had big brown eyes, and lovely auburn hair. She looked like the film star Ava Gardner. She was tall, and towered over my father, who was quite small.'

Anne's mother was born the last of a family of thirteen. She lost her own mother when she was only fourteen. Neither of Anne's parents enjoyed extended formal education, and to the end of their lives, 'Their working class background was strong in them'. Anne's father was a bus driver, who nevertheless was highly literate, and ambitious for his family. Her mother profited from her own father's unusual gifts.

Anne's grandfather was a foreman in the shipyards of her native town, a self-educated man who learned to speak several languages from the sailors he met coming in to the port where he worked. His intelligence made him many important friends who visited the house as Anne's mother was growing up, so she began to form ambitious ideas for her own and her children's lives. She also acquired from her father the confidence to speak out for causes and beliefs that mattered to her, saying, 'What can anyone do to me?' Anne felt her mother was 'naturally undisguised, always herself. At times she was uncompromising, speaking out in ways that made me nervous, but she refused to tone down her remarks if she was convinced she was right in what she believed.'

Anne felt that her mother's emotional and physical strength also derived from her northern roots:

> When I was at school, she'd ask me every day how things were going, and if I told her anything bad – like when I was being bullied, or not given help in catching up with work after an absence, she'd march directly up to the school and tackle the Head face-to-face. She would demand that something was done – that very day. She wouldn't be fobbed off with vague promises. But when the school did put things right, she was also generous in saying 'thank you' to the Head, and even on occasion sending a gift of flowers to express her thanks. I always felt that she was 'in my corner', and because she had such strength, I always felt safe with her.

Anne's mother was possessed of more than confidence in herself. She also, with her husband, had great compassion that was expressed not only in words, but also in direct action. 'As I was growing up, my parents, although far from well off themselves, would sometimes see a poor child whose clothes were ragged and without shoes to her or his feet, and go to the best shop in Hartleypool to buy them decent clothes.'

Anne remembers her parents' marriage as very close and loving. 'My father was quiet and adoring. She was his total life and his source of strength.' They had been childhood sweethearts. Anne believes that the reason she is an only child is that her mother had a very difficult pregnancy with her, and so Anne's father had refused to allow her to put herself at risk with another pregnancy. He was totally absorbed in her, and very possessive.

Even when he was seventy-six, he was capable of being fanatically jealous. I remember one occasion when he thought she was spending too much time talking to another man, and he called me out of the room and made me call her away. My mother was not amused, and said 'I'll talk to whomever I please!'

I think that because mother lost her own mother as a teenager, it was difficult for her to express feelings in words. She didn't have words like 'You look pretty' or 'I love you' when I was growing up. When I was little, that sometimes made me feel unsure of myself and how she felt about me. Although she didn't use words to show how she felt about me, I learned very early that it isn't words that count. For example, I had meningitis when I was fourteen, and she stayed eight hours in the hospital with me every single day. I fully understood even then that her actions were speaking to me. She was saying to me, 'You don't need words – I am here with you'.

This was the gift she gave me. I used to think I was more like my father, but now she is gone, I have come to recognise that I am more like her.

Ana

Ana is a medical practitioner, 'a family doctor' as she likes to be described, who came from Zanzibar in East Africa. Like A. she came to live in England because of her marriage – in her case to an Irishman. She is a ball of energy, with words and ideas spilling out and interspersed with a huge infectious laugh. She conveys instant warmth as she speaks. She says, 'I wasn't really either my mother's or my father's little girl. I was very wild as a child, and loved to take risks.' She has recently broken through an important barrier by becoming the first black woman elected to a very senior ceremonial and public role which until very recently was the almost exclusive preserve of white aristocratic males.

Ana was educated in a strict Catholic convent in Zanzibar, and went to Trinity College Dublin in Ireland to study medicine. While there, she lived in a women's hostel run by nuns. She feels that although her parents were ambitious for her, they left it to her to make a choice of career, and supported her fully when she chose the long hard route to medicine for which she had to leave Zanzibar and her family, as there was no medical school there. On the advice of the Catholic priests, she chose to apply to Dublin, and was accepted on the medical course there.

Ana's mother was born in Goa, but was sent away from her parents to Zanzibar at the time of her arranged marriage to Ana's father, who, like her, was a Catholic. Ana praises her mother's achievements.

She didn't have much education – her father was a ship's cook – but she was very intelligent and a successful businesswoman. Her husband's father, my paternal grandfather had migrated from Goa to Zanzibar as a young man. Although my parents' marriage was arranged, they were devoted to each other, and were partners in running their business as well as their family. They shared a determination to do well, to create a good life for the family, and to see their children succeed in life.

Ana's father had only a modest job at the English Country Club, but the young couple saved every penny they could spare to build up some capital. With their savings, they bought land, investing in first one fruit plantation then another, and later a third with mangoes imported from Goa. As their prosperity grew, they opened a hotel and became the sole importers of a popular German beer.

Throughout these entrepreneurial activities, Ana's mother was a full and successful partner, of whom her daughter was and is proud. Ana recalls:

> She was in charge of all the catering for the business – in the hotel and bar, and for all the staff on the plantations. When my father had a road accident, she took over the entire business and ran it successfully until he recovered.
>
> She was very religious, and had high standards of politeness and general behaviour. We children went home from school for lunch every day, and had strict times for meals. We always had dinner all together. She wanted us all to be very tidy and used to threaten to 'get the broom out' to us if we weren't. She was very much a family person. Her message was to keep the family together always. We used to say the family rosary together. She was very proud of my sister and me because we did so well in school.

Ana has good memories of her mother.

> Before I went to bed to say my prayers each night, I used to try to make her laugh and tell me funny stories. I loved her laugh. I remember the best part of every year was when we had a month in our bungalow by the sea. All the family were together, and we just had great fun. The British forces used to come to the town to play their bands and put on shows. Mother loved the theatre, and went to every play.
>
> Mother was a very kind and caring person. She loved playing the hostess and having lots of visitors. She had known difficult times herself, so she looked after the underprivileged as well. We had a van for the plantations, and we used to collect lots of the oranges in the van and give them out to the poor people on the way as we drove home. We also had one of the very few ice-cream-making machines, and we used to make lots and give it away to poor people.

Like many daughters, Ana remembers especially strongly the enjoyment of shared contact with her mother. 'She was a very good-looking woman, five foot five inches tall. I used to cut her hair for her, and I loved to play with her hair. For herself, she

36

was very keen on fashion, and had seven sets of golden jewellery. She loved to dress up with big earrings and she had lots of extravagant hats. She wanted me to wear make-up, but I said there was no need.'

Ana was the second of her mother's children. She had five sisters and three brothers. Despite her mother's constant pregnancies, such matters were not considered suitable to discuss with her children. 'Mother never talked to us about her pregnancies. We were never told a new baby was coming and never told when it was going to happen. Mother worked to the end of all her pregnancies, and breastfed all her babies. The babies were delivered by the local midwives who were very much of the old school.' The doctor in Ana comments, 'I don't think Mother had very sophisticated care'.

Tragically, Ana's mother died at the birth of the ninth child, at the age of only forty, when Ana herself was just seventeen. As she sadly says, 'I had such a short time with her, only seventeen years'. Those years have remained decisive for her, and decades on, Ana's mother is still a very real presence in her life. 'I pray for her soul.'

Chapter Four
Early Memories: Mummy and Me

There is a special chemistry in a household where mothers and daughters have their own secret life. This is described graphically in Anita Diament's book *The Red Tent*, which tells the story of the women of the House of Jacob and their life in the desert and plains of the Middle East in ancient times. Dinah, the only daughter of Jacob and Leah, is the central character. She has her own brief entry in the book of Genesis in the Bible, where her short marriage and the vengeance of her father and brothers taken on her husband is all that is recorded. Anita Diament, however, focuses on Dinah's childhood and early womanhood as part of the women's life in the red tent – the women's tent no man can enter. Here they retreat during menstruation; here their babies are born. Most important, though, it is here that the stories and traditions peculiar to the life of the women of the tribe are passed on from mother to daughter, generation after generation. The parallel life of the women, as proud and as separate as that of the men, is a precious tradition which provides a vital strength and continuity to the tribe.

Leah, wife of the patriarch Jacob, tells her daughter Dinah the secret of the women's strength. She tells her of the 'Great Mother', the Goddess Innana, who has given to women the secret of menstrual blood. This is a joy to women, she tells her, because it is a sign of their ability to bring new life. The men believe it is pain and bother, and the women let them believe this so that they can continue to retire each month to the red tent and rest, sharing their stories and strengthening their bonds with each other. Leah later fears that this strength is being lost, as the generation of women who are her daughters-in-law allow men to control their lives. They shut away their daughters when they menstruate, as if in shame, denying them the tradition and teaching which came from the shared company of women, forgetting the gift of Innana.

In some of the stories we hear from the women I interviewed there is a sense of this heritage of women. Peggy from Chapter Three and Simone, below, each describe, in very different circumstances, the 'women's world' in which part of their childhood was spent and which exerted a strong influence on their adult lives. Diament says that if you want to understand any woman you must ask about her mother. In the red tent, the mothers told their daughter their stories 'to keep their own memories alive' as well as to give them guidelines for their adult lives. The strength of the life of women and the cohesion of their society, as well as the acceptance of female sexuality as the joy and fulfilment of women's lives, gave to a girl growing up an immense courage and security in her own identity.

Today, we often try to convince ourselves we are breaking free of a mother who is actually a creature of our own invention. We invest her with characteristics we wish to reject and so fail to see the debt we owe for the many qualities we most cherish in ourselves. Nancy Friday's ground-breaking book of the 1970s *My Mother, My Self* examined the difficulty daughters experience in trying to break free of the symbiotic mother-baby relationship, to see their mothers, and their mother's life story as something separate from which they can learn. Once we have become separate, Friday argues, we can give to each other a richer life, drawn from the abundance of our own lives.

In *Fierce Attachments* Vivian Gornick also talks of the world of women in which she grew up in her New York tenement. All she remembers, she says, although the men came and went, to work and to their own interests and lives, is that the tenement was full of women. It was that world of women in which she grew up as a girl, absorbing their values and anxieties, their fear and disdain for men, understanding the 'bargain they had struck' with the limited lives they led.

For various reasons, five of the women to whom I spoke had

always been closer to their mothers than to their fathers. In some cases the father was absent, through separation or divorce, the nature of his work, or illness; in others the social patterns of their family had made their fathers remote figures. The closeness of mother and daughter in these stories is remarkable and moving.

Many women speak of their mother's religious faith, and how this was talked about or learnt in childhood. Ana treasures the gift of her Catholic faith which was such an important part of her mother's life. A. recalls her mother's devotion in the Parsee religion, which still has deep meaning for her. Helen feels that her mother and she are bound together above all else by their Jewish identity. Judith too feels that she and her mother, although in different ways, shared a faith which was important in their lives. For Jinny, her own faith derives from the simple but strong faith which her mother showed in every aspect of her life.

Simone

Tall and dynamic with dramatic red hair, and striking in manner and appearance, Simone presents to the observer as a woman who knows exactly what she wants of life. Now a senior government adviser, manager of a large institution and also a trained counsellor, she grew up in considerable poverty in a small Scottish mining village, where her parents had what she describes as a 'seriously bad time'. One of her siblings had been born dead, and one brother was born after Simone. Simone herself was a weak newborn, weighing only three pounds, and she was put in an incubator at birth. Her mother told her how frantic she had become after the birth, asking where her baby was, and fearing that she had had a second stillbirth.

Simone's 'quiet and sober' father died after eight years of serious illness when Simone was in her teens. Simone's mother nursed and cared for her husband throughout his illness, but later had to go out to work to keep the family. What Simone observed was that her mother's move out of the housewife role 'restored her to herself'. At the same time, her father's death meant that she, her twelve-year-old brother and her mother banded together as a tight-knit threesome. 'We helped each other keep the image we had of ourselves.' This bonding remained throughout the years ahead.

Simone's mother was one of ten children, five of whom were born before her mother's twentieth birthday. Her mother, Simone's grandmother, came from a Jewish family who had rejected her when – at a very young age – she married a non-Jewish husband. Simone's mother was a very bright and able child who passed the examination to go to grammar school at the age of eleven. Sadly though, her family could not afford to send her there, with all the additional expense of uniform, equipment and school outings which they envisaged such attendance would entail. Indeed, the only career planned for her was to 'go into service' with a wealthy family nearby. She rebelled against this prospect, however, and ran away from home. She trained as a nurse, and was proud of her profession, returning to it with joy when she became the sole support of her family.

When asked to describe her mother, Simone asks

Which Mum? My mother was many different people. There was a 'sad mum', the woman who wanted to escape from the confines of her life in the small village where people resented her attractive slim figure, her waistline black hair, her sparkling spirit and defiance of convention. She was even the first woman in the village to wear trousers – a deliberate challenge to the rules, which may have won secret admiration from the men of the village, but which raised doubts amongst many of the respectable women and wives who saw her as a threat to their precarious order. Because she was widowed while still an attractive young woman of thirty-eight, she was excluded from the 'couples' culture' of the suspicious community around her.

For Simone the symbol of this mother was 'my memory of her staring out of the window of our little terraced house, gazing towards England, which she thought of as freedom'. That mum stays in Simone's heart, and in her own way of tackling life, to this day.

Secondly, there was a 'fun mum', the one who entered into her children's games with gusto, and gave their lives joy and meaning. 'I remember her building a tent out of sheets in the living room, and playing "House" with us. I also remember the exciting world of women's secrets, of which Mum was the centre. Because of her nurse's training, she would provide help to women with their pregnancies. It wasn't until later that I realised she had probably also helped many with their need for abortions in those days before the contraceptive pill and legalised abortion.' She was, says Simone, a sort of 'centre for an underground feminist movement concerned with pregnancy and abortion'. This 'mum' introduced Simone to the world of women and their enslavement to the fears of poverty and unwanted pregnancy, indeed to the domination of biological events in the lives of women from her generation.

There was also a 'happy, liberated mum', who appeared when she went back to work, after taking a refresher course to re-register as a nurse. Simone found it a very happy thing that 'she and I could then both study together, I for my school exams and she for her nursing exams'. The lesson that the young Simone learnt was undoubtedly that happiness for a woman came in work and identity outside the home, not from the drudgery of housework and poverty.

Simone also recalls another mother. 'I remember a party where my mother was wearing a taffeta dress, and she was chatting animatedly, and flirting happily. I couldn't get her attention – suddenly I wasn't important to her. That frightened me.' The significance of this incident may perhaps be one with which many women identify. The first time our mothers exhibit their separate, adult, and sexual identity in which we have no part is one that appears in many daughters' recollections and is often a frightening element of their memories of their mothers. Few understand it so well as does Simone.

Simone finds the story of her mother's life is one that has profoundly influenced her.

For a long time, I did things for her. I went to the very same Academy where she had won a place but been unable to go. I was the first in my family ever to go to university, and when it came time for me to leave home and go, it was a very hard time for us both. I found it terribly hard to leave her, but I realised that for her, it was like another death: she felt she was losing me, and she was terribly upset. We had lots of awful arguments in the two years before I left, but I kept telling her that I would be back. I told her that I would send her money – and I did. I even sent her half of my tiny student grant.

I so wish, now, that I'd found the courage to say 'I love you and I don't want to leave you; but I can't stay'. I wish that she had found a way to say to me, 'I love you and I don't want you to go, but I know you must'. Instead, all we did was argue about other and irrelevant things. In part of her heart, she knew I had to go. She was so proud of me, and bragged about what I was doing to the whole village. I wanted to learn, and she loved it.

Jinny

Jinny is a leading educationalist who, for the past twenty years, has travelled around the world as an adviser to governments on education policy and organisation. In the U.K., she has worked with parliamentary committees and various non-departmental bodies. In her youth she was blonde and still has the blue eyes and clear skin with which nature endowed her. Cheerful but thoughtful in manner, she appears a woman at peace with herself and content with her life. She describes herself as 'placid' and claims that her husband has never seen her lose her temper. Unlike many of the women interviewed, she always identified with her mother, and has not a single 'bad' memory of her or of their relationship. For Jinny, her mother was a totally positive role model. 'She was my rock. Nothing happened in my life that she wasn't there.'

Jinny's mother came from a modest background, and although she won a place at grammar school, she left at fifteen. In talking of her mother's life before she herself was born, Jinny recalls, 'Her father was very ambitious for his daughter. He was a railwayman, self educated, but very well educated.' Jinny's mother was one of three children, and her brother was killed in the Second World War. Her sister, Jinny's aunt, was very academic, and pursued an academic career. 'She was often slightly scornful of my mother, and of me,' Jinny recalls, 'but my mother always stood up for me and what I could achieve'.

One such occasion was when Jinny decided to apply to a prestigious institution for her higher education.

My aunt poured scorn on the idea, and said, 'You'll never get accepted there!' but my mother was determined that I should, and could. She had faith in me, and that made me have faith in myself. I did get accepted, and although my brother was cleverer that I am, and went to Oxford, neither of my parents ever made me feel that I should be like him. In fact, my brother always felt that I could persuade our parents better than he could. He used to say, 'You ask them – they'll do it for you'.

Jinny's respect for her mother includes a slight awe of her gift of second sight. 'My mother was psychic in the most extraordinary way. The night her brother was killed in the war, she ''saw'' him on the staircase of the family home. She knew something was wrong, and the next day the news of his death came. Even after my marriage, when she visited our home, she would sometimes ''see'' the former owner there.'

Talented and gifted as Jinny's mother unquestionably was, her life for the first twenty years of her marriage to Jinny's father, a successful jeweller, was to be one of amazing self-sacrifice. Immediately after her marriage, and when she and Jinny's father had just bought their first house, her mother became ill. Without complaint, she and her new husband moved, with his support and agreement, into her parents' home to care for her invalid mother. The family remained there for twenty years, all the years of Jinny and her brother's childhood.

Jinny pays tribute to her father's role in this, but it is her mother's sacrifice she now remembers. 'She never, ever complained. Any evening when she and Daddy went out, she would return on the dot of ten to put my grandmother to bed. She never, in all those years, saw the end of a play or film. She was a slave to the family. Although she was a woman of deep faith, she never even came to church with us on Sunday mornings, because she had to stay to cook the Sunday lunch. She used to tell me that God understood that it was her duty.'

Despite her constricted life, Jinny's mother never failed to give her children the fun and attention they needed.

Without the benefit of any formal training in education through play, Mummy used to provide us with all the best play materials, including a sand-pit and toys to use with it. She encouraged us to dress up and act. I remember on one occasion when we were dressing up, my brother made me a mask and then decided that I needed to have my fringe cut off to make it look right. I thought Mummy would be furious, but she wasn't, she just laughed. She was a wonderful mother and a totally selfless woman.

It is with affection and amusement that Jinny recalls the only time when she can remember her mother being very cross. 'My grandmother's house was a big house, with an orchard and a large garden leading down to the rail tracks. There was a railway bridge just at the foot of the garden, and one of the absolute rules was that we were never, ever to go under the bridge. On this one occasion, my brother and I decided to disobey the rules, and go down under the bridge. It was filthy and muddy and we literally got ''stuck in the mud''. We had to shout for someone to rescue us. It was the only time I saw her really furious. I suppose she thought of all the terrible things that could have happened to us. But at least we never did that again!'

Jinny's education in sexual matters was adequate, and perhaps less restricted than that of many girls of her generation and class. She does, however, well recall special moments with her mother when she felt secure in raising her questions. 'I used to sit on the edge of the bath talking to her after my bath, and one time she began to talk to me to explain what masturbation was. I said, ''Oh, I know all about that, but what I do want to know is what do lesbians do?'' Mummy wasn't shocked, she just laughed and said she didn't know either!'

Later, however, her innocence even as a young student appears in the story of what happened when Jinny had met her future husband. 'While I was visiting my brother at Oxford, he left me alone for a few minutes with his best friend. At that time, we were just casual friends. As soon as we were alone, he came over to where I was standing and kissed me. I was rather shocked, and thought perhaps this wasn't right. When I told my mother, and said I had been shocked, she said I should know that such an approach wasn't necessarily a bad thing. It probably just meant he liked me a lot.' The older Jinny now reflects, 'How typical of our relationship, both that I should tell her, and that instead of laughing at me, she should help me understand.'

Jinny remembers a conversation with her mother which still has meaning for her today. 'One day when I was seven, I went to talk to my Mother in the kitchen. I was very sad about my grandmother, and how crippled she was with arthritis. I said, "Why don't we pray for Grandma to get better?" Her wise answer was, "Let's pray together to say to God that if it's right for Grandma to get better, then He should make her better but please to make her life easier, even if she can't get well." What a tactful answer to give to a little seven-year-old.'

Jinny freely acknowledges the debt she owes to her mother. The closeness they enjoyed, and the support that she received permeated her life. She, like so many successful women, remembers her mother's determination to give her 'the very best' of everything. 'When I went away to college, Mummy was determined that I should have everything new. She collected clothing coupons (which we needed in those post-war days) and got the most wonderful things for me. She was so proud of me, and I think I fulfilled all her hopes. I never, ever doubted that I was loved.'

Poppy

Poppy is a former nurse and trained counsellor married to a senior international businessman. She is tall and elegant, with striking dark brown eyes and hair and one is immediately struck by the animation in her face and voice and in the way she moves. She describes, with unnecessary modesty, her formal career as a 'sideline'. Nevertheless, her success as a full-time partner in the demanding social side of her husband's international business life represents achievement every bit as significant in its way as her success in the career she has pursued in her own right. Perhaps because of her training as a counsellor, she is able to exercise a high degree of self-awareness in talking of her relationships.

Poppy talks of her mother with warm affection, but with a degree of both criticism and understanding. 'Mummy was Swedish, and so different from everyone else's mother. She looked distinctive, very good looking – striking in fact.' Poppy's mother grew up in a wealthy and aristocratic household. 'She was a dedicated royalist and admired all things English. Her upbringing in Sweden in the early ears of the twentieth century did not prepare her for anything much beyond the role of wife, hostess and mother.'

Poppy's childhood was one of travel with her parents and a degree of separation from them. Of her mother she says,

I always wanted her to be warmer than she was. She didn't have many friends, and didn't invite my friends to our house. She was very unworldly, aristocratic in fact, and never worked a day in her life. They lived abroad a lot, and she was just totally loyal to my father. He was very autocratic, but underneath he was a 'touchy-feely' kind of man. Her total loyalty bothered me. I wanted her to stand up to him. Their marriage lasted only because Mummy was subservient. It would never have lasted any other way.

I feel, though, that I've done the same as she did. I've followed my husband's career and very seldom done anything in my own right. I have no regrets about that. His career has always generated enough to keep me busy, and I've always tried to have sidelines – teaching English as a foreign language when we lived abroad, and then working as a marriage counsellor more intensively in later years.

Poppy feels that her parents achieved a sense of security for their children, despite many periods of separation. 'Mummy was always just "there" and I know she loved me. I felt very secure in being loved by them both. I didn't have a good enough relationship with my father to talk to him very much. I was always closer to Mummy than to Daddy.'

Like many of the women in this book, Poppy reflects on the sexual undertones of her parents' marriage.

My father definitely 'fancied' me. He never made a pass, or acted inappropriately, but he talked to me about how frigid Mummy was. He told me that their sex life was unsatisfactory. I also didn't feel it was appropriate when he gave me advice about personal hygiene. It was he who cried all the way through my wedding! I wanted Mummy to do more things with me. Even when I was due to be married, we didn't do any of those mother-daughter girlie things like choosing the wedding dress and shopping for a trousseau.

Some aspects of her mother's parenting still seem bizarre to Poppy, an independent woman, very much at home in the era of constant international travel. 'I left home at seventeen, and went to do my training as a nurse. I was very independent, and fended for myself, but I asked Mummy why she didn't come to England to visit me while she and Daddy were living in Finland, which is really not so far away. She said she would never be brave enough to travel without Daddy, and couldn't possibly have come to England without him. I don't think she was a good mother in that.'

Poppy was born early in the Second World War, and her first years were spent in neutral Sweden alone with her mother. She has distant but happy memories of those early times when they were together, times which did not come again until the last few years of her mother's life.

Poppy undoubtedly had years of separation and distance from her mother in the years when she was growing up, but these have faded in her memory now in the light of the adult years they spent together after her father's death. Poppy now sums up the relationship she had with her mother in saying simply, 'I feel great about Mummy'.

Helen

Helen is a senior medical consultant, the first of our women whose parents were divorced when she was a small child. She is lively, energetic, quick of mind and humour, with curly fair hair, now greying, and twinkling blue eyes, which must have been of great cheer to her many patients. Helen is thoughtful and self-aware, speaking of her early childhood memories of her mother with deep affection and understanding. She is also keen to point out that because of the circumstances of her life, an evacuee during the war years and child of a working single mother, she feels that she was raised more by others than by her own mother. 'I didn't feel that Mummy did raise me. Lots of other people, aunts, my grandmother, the people I stayed with for a year in Wales without Mummy, they were all just as important in raising me and offering role models.' The bond, however, is still there, unmistakable, and unbreakable, and the things said and unsaid are as real, as happy and as painful as in relationships acknowledged to be much closer.

Helen's mother was born into an orthodox Jewish family in Warsaw, Poland, in 1910. She was one of ten children, of whom only six survived into adulthood. Her father was the headmaster of a small Jewish school (Jews were not allowed into Polish state schools), and during the First World War the family had a very hard time indeed. Helen's mother would tell later of how the entire family had shared one egg as their meal on more than one occasion.

The family moved to England in 1919. By now father was seriously asthmatic, and constantly ill. Tragically, one daughter – one of a pair of twins – died soon after the move to England, and this loss was a terrible blow. Helen says, 'For my grandmother, the clock just stopped ticking when that daughter died. She became totally deaf, and shortly afterwards was devastated by a further blow, when one of her sons who had remained in Poland, giving his passport to a brother of military service age, died there.'

Despite this unhappy beginning, the remaining family settled in England well enough. Helen's mother did well at school, and went on to train as a dressmaker. She soon became a highly skilled dress designer, and in 1929, at the age of just nineteen, she married Helen's father, a happy-go-lucky man, who, alas, proved incapable of settling down to any sort of responsibility. On one occasion, Helen's mother suffered the indignity of the arrival of bailiffs who came to take all the family furniture in payment of the unpaid bills. Only one wooden box was left in the house. As any money he made was instantly frittered away, his wife had no choice but to go out to work to support herself and her baby daughter. Helen's memories of her mother, therefore, from the very earliest days, are of a working mother, who both earned and guarded the family income.

Her mother's success as a designer, and her ambition for herself and her daughter meant that Helen enjoyed private education in her early years. Her mother also brought in a maid to help in the home, but this proved a tragic mistake. The maid was young and, before many months had gone by, Helen's father ran away with one of her pretty young friends. From that day, Helen was to see her father only three or four times in the rest of her life.

Helen and her mother had a few years of unsettled life, living with Helen's uncle for a while, and finally settling in South Wales, where Helen's mother had found a good job in a dress factory, and Helen entered her fifth school at the age of nine. It was there that her mother fell in love and married for the second time. Helen acquired a stepfather, a Dutch serviceman in the Free Dutch army, whom she grew to love greatly (she calls him Father). He brought with him two stepbrothers and a stepsister for Helen, the children of his previous marriage. He was to prove a good father to her, and a devoted husband to her mother.

Helen pays tribute to the way her mother handled the matter of her engagement. 'She handled her marriage to Father very well. Before she would agree to an engagement, she made sure that he and I had got to know each other and had become good friends. She told me they were to be married only when she was sure that I was happy about him.'

The marriage, though, was to bring one major unwelcome change in Helen's mother's life. In order for her new husband to be allowed custody of his children, and to bring them out of occupied Holland to England, he had to make a solemn declaration that they would be raised in a Christian family, in the Christian tradition. Helen and her mother therefore had to forgo all their Jewish identity, 'Until the day Father died, when Mummy was seventy-one, she never again acknowledged her Jewish faith publicly. From the day he died, however, she became Jewish again.'

Helen felt that all these events meant that for many years she was not given priority in her mother's life. 'She was always so busy during the war, and then there was the distraction of Father's children coming to live with us. We had different priorities. Hers was her marriage: mine was my study and my career. I don't feel my Mother had any part in my achievements. She worked long hours and wasn't really able to relate to my experience.'

Helen recognises some of the influence of her mother's view of life on how she sees herself as an adult.

My mother and her Jewish family just accepted discrimination from their early days in Poland, and then later my mother had to give up her religion in order for Father to have his children with him. I have adopted that acceptance completely. I think to myself, that if I can't fight it, I don't bother. I have never tried to do things I really wanted if I felt that prejudice would prevent me getting there. I have inherited the trait of giving in to things; for example, I never protested that when I went to medical school, there was a quota both for women and for Jews. I just accepted it.

Helen tries to minimise her mother's influence on her life in much of what she says, yet emphasises the importance of their relationship.

My relationship with my mother was uneasy – not a good relationship. I disagreed with her whenever I could and I was 'uppity' to her. I wanted to be different from her although I now realise that in a real sense I am like her in lots of ways. I still feel uncomfortable with that, though. I get my intolerance from her, but then again, I also get the habit of spending time with my nose in a book from her. My life is lived inside myself, and hers wasn't.

Helen's Jewish identity remains an important and defining part of her adult identity, and of her feelings, perhaps unacknowledged, towards her mother.

My Jewish identity was a problem for me, made worse by the fact that Mummy and I had to conceal it for Father's sake

51

after he had promised he was married to a Christian in order to get his children with him. Being Jewish inside has always made me feel an outsider, and I think Mummy longed to be able to be with her Jewish family, and to acknowledge who she was all those years, even though it was a sacrifice she made for Father's sake, and for her marriage. Although I never attend a synagogue in this country, and have no memory of ever being a practising Jew, I really only feel at home when I attend a Liberal Orthodox service in Australia with my uncles and their families.

As with so many of the women in this story, Helen's love of her mother shines through the many conflicting thoughts of her.

I was very proud of Mummy. She was so pretty, creative, clever – and happy and pleasant to be with. I liked her laugh! When we were at the cinema, she would go on laughing at the funny bits in films long after everyone else. We were very close, and never let our differences get in the way. I feel no identity with her as a woman although physically I can see the resemblance. I loved her.

Jane

Jane, whose parents were also separated when she was a teenager, is well known in the field of development studies, where she has published groundbreaking research. A distinguished researcher with a first degree from Cambridge and a doctorate from the London School of Economics, she has advised governments in the developing world about their agricultural and irrigation schemes, and is a regular traveller to remote parts of the world. Confident and impressive in her own area of expertise, Jane is also an accomplished hostess, and tends to be chosen as a natural organiser in any group, whether in her home town or travelling with an overseas mission. She is an outstanding example of a wife and mother who managed to build a successful name and niche for herself despite the constant moves around the world demanded by her husband's career.

Her story is of two remarkable lives – her own and her mother's. Together they provide a fascinating example of strong-willed, determined and brave women, whose lives and personalities have much in common, and yet whose relationship was never easy. Jane herself describes it as 'a slightly ambivalent relationship. I admired Mummy for her fighting spirit, but we were so different.' Nevertheless, Jane acknowledges the bond between them in certain ways, not least their immense strength of character. She also acknowledges her mother's encouragement. 'Mummy trusted me. She knew that I was clever and always encouraged me in my education and to have a career.'

Jane's mother was one of ten children born in China into an aristocratic English family, performing their duties in peacekeeping around the world and in what was then the British Empire. While she lived abroad with her parents in Asia as a small child, she lost both her little sister and her father when she was only eight years old. The family then returned to England, and she was sent to St Swithin's, the school that became a byword for the upper-class girls' schools of the early twentieth century, and also one of the pioneers of girl's education in the nineteenth century. Jane's mother's family had a strong tradition of valuing education, and she carried on this tradition in the way she encouraged her two daughters in their education, broken as it was by the traumas of the Second World War.

Jane has the good fortune to have been left with an unpublished autobiography written by her mother. 'I am lucky to have the book she left. It is a story and record of her life, and tells how she felt. I think you only begin to understand some of your mother's feelings when you become a mother yourself.' The book describes how desperately unprepared for marriage and a sexual relationship Jane's mother was. 'As my grandmother was seeing my parents off on their honeymoon at the end of the wedding, she took my father to one side and said to him, "Be gentle with her, she doesn't know a thing". As she had ten children of her own one would think that she might have been a little more helpful in preparing my mother. Still, as far as one can tell, my parents seem to have coped at that stage.'

Jane's parents separated when she was fourteen, and her memories are of a working mother both before and after the separation.

We were living in Hong Kong during the early part of the war, and my sister and I had a Chinese nurse, who looked after us while Mummy was busy with a lot of voluntary work. We were evacuated to Australia when Hong Kong fell in 1941, and while we lived there Mummy was a full-time mother for a short time. Then we moved to India to be near my father, and she threw herself into voluntary work with the British troops, running a canteen, and rushing around on her bicycle.

Jane's memory of the period leading up to the separation is the stuff of amazing fiction.

My father left the Royal Air Force at the end of the War to become a Colonel in the British army in Burma, to help with the repatriation of British troops there. Mummy also wanted to help, and asked to go to Hong Kong, where we had still many friends, to help with the repatriation going on there. She left my little sister and me in India, and had arranged for someone to come and look after us while she was gone. Unfortunately the carer never turned up, so although I was just fourteen, I was left to deal with the servants, paying them off at the end of their time with us. The first thing that happened was that I broke my elbow and then I developed chickenpox in the middle of all this. I knew that if the servants saw the rash they would abandon us and run off, so I put camomile lotion on my face to cover the rash and carried on. I never had proper treatment for the elbow, and it is still crooked now.

Mummy sent a message to tell me to pack up all our possessions and arrange for them to be shipped to Bombay. She then sent another message to say she was coming by boat to Bombay and would meet us there. She didn't quite say when she would arrive, and so when my sister and I got off the train in Bombay and unloaded all our big crates of possessions, there was no one there to meet us. We didn't know what to do. By a lucky coincidence, my father had arrived in Bombay that day, and our aunt had told him that we were coming in on the train, so after what seemed like hours, he arrived at the station to try to find us. My mother's boat docked later that day and we all met up at my aunt's house. It was there, on that same day, that my father told my mother that their marriage was over. He had met a Burmese woman, and wanted to marry her. My mother never granted him a divorce, though.

Jane does not believe that the Burmese woman was the real reason for the break-up of her parents' marriage. She feels that the real cause was the death of their only son in a tragic road accident when he was a teenager and Jane was only four. 'Both my parents were devastated by their loss, but for my mother, we two girls were some consolation. For my father, though, we were never of any equal value. The family was dead for him. He never really showed any great interest in us again.'

Although Jane was only four when her brother died, she has an indelible memory of how her mother broke the news to her – an exchange which has frequently come back to her in coming to terms with her mother's death. It is a memory which speaks both of her mother's faith, and of the loving care she had for her daughter, even at a time of devastating grief of her own.

Mummy took me into John's bedroom, and showed me the box where my brother had been keeping some caterpillars from the garden. 'Look' she said, 'remember those caterpillars John collected? They all turned into the rather dead looking chrysalises, didn't they? Well, those are gone now too.' She took me over to the window with the box in my hands and opened the window. 'Now' she said 'open the box. Do you see? They have turned into these beautiful white cabbage butterflies. Let them out and watch them fly away. See how happy and how free they are? It's just like that for John. We won't see him again, but he is free and happy now.'

I have never forgotten that moment, and I can still see those butterflies fluttering their wings as they flew into the sunshine. It helped me to understand something about how to cope with death, and shows how much she was trying to help me even in the midst of her own grief. She was splendid at that time.

Chapter Five
Work, Sex and Children

Adult Relationships

> Child, I no longer
> need to choose;
> all choices are yours now,
> make them wisely.
> from Wanda Barford, 'To Market'

Growing up is never easy, but there comes a moment in the lives of mother and daughter when each must recognise that the relationship has to adapt and change. The daughter is becoming an adult who must make her own choices and live with her own mistakes. It takes a mature mother and an even more mature daughter to recognise the moment. In her poem 'To Market' Wanda Barford is speaking of a mother who, recognising that moment, gently nudges her daughter away from asking her mother to make choices for her. The final motherly admonition 'make them wisely' is a loving mother wishing her daughter well in her adult and independent life, but refusing – rightly – to make her decisions for her. It is a description of a good and healthy parting from the childhood period of dependency.

Many of us as daughters search for one more experience of hiding from our responsibilities under the wings of motherly protection, long after it is appropriate, and many of us continue to blame our mothers for our choices when they prove wrong. Growing up is never entirely easy, and because of the special nature of the daughter-mother relationship, many women try to build their adult and separate identity using the psychic energy generated by assumed grievances and anger against their mother. Like many women, I found that as an adult I still carried the baggage of my childhood, and the relationship I had with my mother. The strengths and weaknesses of that relationship go with us all, in the choices we make, in a world very different from that of our mothers', about sexual relationships, marriage, career and children. How we deal with this baggage can determine the rightness of our choices as well as our ability to be at peace with ourselves.

The tension generated by difficult relationships between mothers and daughters, in which neither quite breaks free of the other, can be crippling for both. The film *Postcards from the Edge*, in which Meryl Streep and Shirley MacLaine play the parts of mother and daughter, portrays just such a destructive relationship. The daughter refuses to use her singing talent because she has always been overshadowed in this field by her mother's charismatic personality. She feels (not without some justification) that her brilliant and successful mother will always upstage her if she pursues a career in the same area. She can be neither creative nor happy until she makes peace with her mother. This they finally achieve, acknowledging their love for each other but also discovering that the competition in their relationship is two-way. The daughter may feel overshadowed by her mother's success, but her mother is facing fears that her talent and success are fading. She is suffering the pains of getting older and 'past it' and feels envious of her daughter's youth and success. The two women are destroying each other's talent and happiness.

Only when they become honest with each other can they be redeemed by their love for each other. The daughter is able to make full use of her talent – so like and yet so different from her mother's – and is free at last to do what she wants for her own reasons. Her mother, acknowledging her feelings in a moment of understanding and affection, tells her, 'I'm jealous because you still have your chance. Make the most of it.' In a wry recognition of her own youth's limitations she adds, 'At least one of us should enjoy being young'.

Anne Robinson's autobiography *Confessions of an Unfit*

Mother also charts the troubled relationship between herself and her very demanding, high-powered but alcoholic mother. She loves her mother dearly, and recognises that her mother has never failed to 'be there' for her, and yet carries the burden of her mother's behaviour throughout her life. She asks why so often, and secretly, daughters may consider their mother more enemy than friend. Robinson felt throughout much of her adult life that her mother was both controlling her and criticising her, leaving her with self-doubt and guilt which led in turn to her own descent into alcoholism.

Robinson's mother was a businesswoman in the Liverpool of the Second World War era. She cut an impressive figure, terrorising all with whom she did business, making vast sums out of the black market and spending prodigiously on high living for herself and her family. Anne Robinson pays undisguised tribute to her mother's skills in business, and to her devotion to her family. Like Simone, she recognises many different versions of her mother: the stylish and lavish shopper; the unforgiving taskmaster; but above all the 'empowerer'. This is the mother who has given to Anne the strength to fight her way through appalling low points in her life to the peaks of attainment she now scales. Her mother frequently said to her, 'You can go out into the world and do *anything*'.

It is only now, after her mother's death, when Robinson has learned to deal with her life as an independent adult, that she can acknowledge both her love and admiration for her mother's achievements and the debt she owes to her for her strength and determination. She completes her autobiography by rejoicing in the certainty that her mother would have adored her popular programme *The Weakest Link* and would have been delighted by her success.

The relationship between every daughter and mother inevitably changes when the daughter becomes an adult, with her own family and career attachment. It is not surprising that many of the women in the generation with whom we are concerned consciously reject their mother's lifestyle and what they perceive as their mother's wishes for them, since their lifestyle is so very different from what their mothers could have envisaged. As Terri Apter found in her study of adolescent girls, many will work hard to prove that they are different from their mothers, because

the adolescent girl needs to break free, wants to avoid enmesh-
ment in her mother's ways and values. She will often use her
mother as 'a measure of opposites', trying to be everything her
mother was not. Apter observes, though, that in so doing she is
just as tied to the model of her mother as she would be in copying
her: her identification with her mother is still just as strong when
she uses her mother as the model and measure of her difference.

Much modern research has shown that the belief of the feminists in the 1970s that we could create a new generation for our
daughters, women who would make very different life-choices
from those forced too often on our mothers, was in part misplaced.
The sheer force of the mothering instinct outweighs for many
women the other ambitions they have and share with their male
colleagues. Although the generation of young women who are
our daughters feel much less outwardly constrained than we or
our mothers did, many, as we have seen earlier in the research by
Madeleine Arnot and her associates, still make gender-determined
choices, just as their mothers and grandmothers did.

Rosalind Coward, herself a feminist writer of the 1970s, now
explores in her recent radical book *Sacred Cows* how hard women
find it to give up the central role in their children's lives, which
generations of women before them had accepted as the norm.
The women she interviewed had worked, often in exciting and
demanding careers before the birth of their children, and they
experienced all the traditional feminist conflicts of guilt if they
worked and saw less of their children, or guilt if they stayed at
home and relied on their husbands' support. But these women
were no longer constrained by the expectations of society outside;
they were responding to imperatives of their own feelings and
their own wishes for a close bond with their children. In 1993,
Dr Catherine Hakim published her scholarly and surprising
research into young women's choices about their lives, and
reported that less than a third in her sample said they wanted a
'career' and most found that part-time work suited them best.

In *Baby Hunger* Hewlett charts the urgency of the longing for
babies that haunts even the most dedicated career women in her
study. Just as we hear from many of the women interviewed for
this book, it seems that there are imperatives in the female condition which outlast the generations, despite the huge changes

made by the revolution in women's lives which occurred in the 1970s and 1980s. Perhaps, after all, we are not so different from our mothers as for many years we supposed.

Margaret Drabble vividly describes the rejecting daughter in her confessedly autobiographical novel *The Peppered Moth*. Chrissie, who is Drabble's portrayal of herself, dreads becoming like the mother she perceives as unsuccessful, bitter and unhappy. She decides in her late teens that she will not try to be top of her class as her mother Bessie had been, nor, she thinks, will she have anything to do with words, as literature had been her mother's subject at Cambridge, and Chrissie feels she has 'had enough of words'.

Bessie is of the generation which Hannah Gavron describes in *The Captive Wife*. Born into a working-class home in Yorkshire, Bessie was highly intelligent and justly proud of her hard-won Cambridge degree. Marriage and children were for her, as for so many of her generation, an abrupt limit on her own ambition. Although she was married to a successful barrister, she had to confine her own ambition to being a good mother – reading all the latest books on child-rearing and diet – and making herself a very good cook and perfectionist housewife. Frustration led her to suffer from almost permanent depression, and violent outbursts of anger, usually against the members of her family. She was not a model for a happy adult life. Small wonder, then, that Bessie's daughter wanted to be as different as possible from her.

In many ways, though, the book is not only the author's search for her mother, but Drabble's recognition that her desperate resolution to be different was bound to fail. Chrissie was 'programmed' to follow her parents' path in life to a far greater degree than she wished or recognised. Like her mother, she went to Cambridge; like her mother she became a word-person. In the character of Chrissie, Drabble portrays much of herself, and much of her mother is in Bessie, but we the readers know that this author overcame the destiny of repeating her mother's experience of despair, anger and unfulfilled talent. Unlike her unhappy mother, she has been able to use words to write books which captivate and enthral the reader, books which have brought her fame and, one hopes, a measure of the happiness that events denied to her mother.

As we have seen, Vivian Gornick's book *Fierce Attachments* tells of a lifelong failed attempt to communicate between a mother and daughter, with what she describes as a 'no-man's-land' of infinite space between them. Her mother clings to the conviction that life is about the love of one man, and that happy marriage is simply all there is to life. Vivian cannot impress her mother with her feminist views or her success as a writer. Her mother scoffs at her fancy college-educated ideas, and painfully prods at Vivian's failure to make lasting relationships with any man. It is just because Vivian cannot quite rid herself of some inner need to gain her mother's approval – and perhaps some even stronger fear that her mother is right about her – that they are emotionally locked together; the daughter cannot leave her mother, make her own choices or get on with her own life, nor can her mother refrain from mocking all that her daughter achieves.

Vivian also tackles the theme of women's sexuality, and the way in which a daughter's feelings about sex and about men often derive from early experience and her mother's half-heard and half-understood secret conversations with other women. Vivian remembers her childhood in the Bronx tenement as filled with women and the constant talk of sex. Her mother was obsessed by her fear of Vivian's sexuality, and fought against her friendship with some of the women in the tenement who were sexually active and permissive. Sex was often the warring ground for Vivian's fights with her mother – and the crude talk of sex from the women in the tenement determined more of her own attitudes to men, and her inability to maintain a relationship, than she wished to admit. In the partly understood words of these women and the behaviour she observed, Vivian learned of their distrust of men, and the abuse they often accepted from drunken and violent husbands and lovers, as well as their need of men, both material and sexual. She tells her mother later that it was 'sexual rage' which made those women the way that they were.

The women I interviewed for this book tell many different stories of their adult relationships with their mothers. Some speak openly about the sexual element in their family relationships; many report that the subject was never mentioned. Some felt that

61

their mothers approved openly of all the choices they made about their lifestyle, while others are left with huge self-doubt. Did they disappoint their mother? Was the choice they made one which caused her distress? Those who turned away from the life their mother had led sometimes wonder if she saw this as a rejection of her, or whether she rejoiced in the seizing of opportunities denied to her.

Peggy, competing in the world of local politics, was one who rejected what she saw as her mother's life-choices. A happy marriage had been the centrepiece of her mother's life, and she always felt that her own broken marriage was a bitter disappointment to her mother.

I think her greatest ambition for me was to make a good marriage. All my boyfriends had adored her, and my husband became very close to her. When his own mother died, he didn't cry in front of me, but he talked to Mummy, and she cuddled him while he sobbed his grief out in her arms.

She was devastated when my marriage broke up. Her own marriage had been so happy, and she always thought that was what mattered most. I remember after my Dad died, she came to spend Christmas with us. One night I noticed her sitting quietly at dinner with tears streaming down her face, and when she saw me looking at her, she just said 'I miss your Dad'.

I did feel the lack of a happy marriage myself, but I always knew I didn't want *her* kind of happy marriage. I didn't want to be a little housewife, which was how we saw her. But perhaps she wasn't that, after all. She did help me to see that women could be independent. She coped without my father for the war years; she made beautiful clothes for us all, and developed wonderful skills as a cook – making gorgeous baked goods like plum duff, parkin and apple pies. She enjoyed her job at the designer clothes shop, and was very good at it. She and I had a great time as two women together decorating my new house; I stripped the walls and she put up the wallpaper. That was good fun.

Peggy had made her choice, both about the kind of marriage she wanted, and about her career. She pursued her career in local government with healthy ambition, and succeeded in rising to a very senior and prominent position. She feels confident that her mother was proud of these accomplishments.

She was very proud when I got to university, and she followed my career with much interest. She loved my piano playing and kept my piano in her house for years after I married 'just in case I wanted to play'. I had always thought that I got my musical talent from my Dad, and he was the one who took me to operas when I was at school, and sent me to elocution classes to help me with an acting or singing career. I used to give recitals of poetry, and I sang in a youth choir and acted in several amateur plays.

My mother wasn't musical, but she had a lovely singing voice. It wasn't until after her death that I learned that she too had been much admired as a 'reciter' before her marriage.

It took some time for Peggy to feel a mature and adult freedom with her mother but in the last months of their time together, the closeness and happiness of the early years of childhood returned with joy and love.

Anne, living first in a world of business and then academic activity as an anthropologist, also suffered a painful divorce, and felt that her broken marriage was a reflection on her inability to find the happiness that her parents had. Her mother was delighted when she married.

At my wedding she looked beautiful. She wore a wonderful hat and a string of pearls. She adored both my sons, and they adored her. When the younger one was only eighteen months old, my husband ran off with another woman, so I was left to cope. I had no choice but to go into business, and I decided on the property business. I presented the bank with a business plan, which they approved, and so I started up with a loan. It was a very small start! For my first venture I built an annexe on to my house and rented it out. I am glad the business grew so much, as it made it possible for me to bring my sons up in comfort, sending them to good private schools. It also allowed me to support my parents.

Anne sent her parents generous amounts of money to make their lives easier. They never spent it, however. 'They still had their working-class background strong in them, and they wanted to live their own way.' In spite of this, they were pleased at their daughter's successful life. 'My mother was very proud of me, and used to tell all her friends about my successes. She was pleased when I decided to return to academic life.' Anne still has moments of pain about her relationship with her mother, and struggles to come to terms with many aspects of the latter part of her parents' lives. Although she was vividly aware of her parents' strong relationship and love for each other – and indeed of the possessive jealousy her father could feel about his wife and other men – she does not record any open discussion about sex in the family. The failure of her own marriage, however, still seems a painful contrast to the devotion of her parents.

Judith's story is also of a first marriage that ended in divorce. As she joined her parents in their successful retail business she was able to observe her mother's behaviour and skill.

I chose my mother when I chose my husband; he had all her enterpreneurial skills, and her big dreams. I worked in my parents' business, taking my father's role as a cost accountant, and my husband married into the business. When we married, we were running twelve shops supplying just about everything from food to cosmetics.

We built up the business, buying up more stores and moving into the mainstream food business. My husband was the sales-man and I arranged the buying and the transport and so on. Both my parents retired, but I spoke constantly to my father for his advice and approval. My husband spoke constantly to my mother; they got on so well together. After he left me, my parents never spoke to him again. It was the family that mattered to them, as always. When I parted from my husband, we split the business on a fifty-fifty share. He started playing dangerous games with his half, and I was afraid the business would start to decline, so I sold my half and went to work for a subsidiary of the company that had bought my company.

Mummy adored my son. After my divorce, she made him the centre of her life. She was delighted when I married again.

She thought it wonderful that I had a husband who was rich and would take care of me. My second husband endeared himself to my father by asking his permission for my hand in marriage. Sadly, he became ill just after the wedding and died of cancer shortly afterwards. My mother advised me never to marry again. She told me I now had everything I needed, money and position, and I should just carry on with my life without a husband.

Judith's memory of her mother and the red cami-knickers which her father had given his wife reveals the strong element of sexuality in her parents' marriage. Judith remarked that she had always felt some sense of competition with her mother for her father's love, speaking honestly as the little girl who wished for her father's attention to be directed towards her and not her mother. Such feelings are so often an unspoken and unrecognised part of the family dynamic. For a girl growing up, the approval and love she receives from her father can determine her confidence in boy-girl and man-woman encounters later on. More than anything her mother can contribute, a father can give to his daughter confidence in relationships with the opposite sex. Judith reports, however, her admiration for the care her mother lavished on her father in the last years of his life, demonstrating a relationship which matured healthily through her adult years.

A. sadly left her mother behind in India when she came to England with her English husband. Her marriage too broke up after several years.

My mother thought the world of my husband. We never talked about my divorce at the time it happened; she never said a word. She did understand, and she loved me, but she was very, very sad. Although she adored him, he was always very scathing about her. I never told her, of course, but he said cruel things about her. She had late-onset diabetes, and was often ill. Once she went into a diabetic coma when she was staying with us in England, and my husband just said that she was making everyone suffer for her illness. She didn't deserve to suffer for so long. She was such a good and generous person.

A. feels that she is to blame for having deprived her mother of the joy of watching her granddaughter grow up. Although they visited India many times, and her mother came to England to visit them, she missed the day-to-day contact with A.'s daughter that she would have loved. 'I felt I had cheated her,' A. says sadly.

For her part. A. too missed the regular contact with her mother, and the sharing of her daughter's childhood.

She was such a beautiful knitter, and when I was expecting my baby, I felt I wanted something knitted by my mother for my child. I sent her some patterns and some wool so that when I brought my baby out of hospital she was wearing a complete set of woollies made by my mother. She and my daughter were very close. Even in her last years when she went blind, she always knew when my daughter was in the room.

I think she had to fight off the sadness that I left her to go to England. I was also marrying 'out' of the Parsee community, but she was very open-minded and didn't object to that. She was a devout Parsee, but didn't talk about it a great deal, it was just central to her life.

As A. says this, she is moved by a realisation of the gulf between her mother's life and her own. 'I live in such a different environment from the one I grew up in as a girl.'

A. feels that her mother faced suffering and death with tremendous courage. 'She was ill for so long, and her blindness was very difficult. She often said she would like to die, but that she just had to keep on doing all she could. Every time I said goodbye to her at the end of a visit I knew it could be for the last time.'

A. had been given a model of a happy marriage by her parents, but had also had a model from her mother of the ability to carry on alone after her father's early death. This undoubtedly gave A. the strength to build up her own business career after her divorce. The closeness the two women found in the last years of her mother's life has been a source of comfort to A., but as we shall see later, she found the loss of her mother most hard to bear, and still feels guilt and regret for many aspects of her life.

Peggy, Anne, Judith and A. all describe themselves as Daddy's girls, as does Ana, who had virtually no adult life with her mother, since she lost her when she was only seventeen. She was far away from her home in Zanzibar, studying for her medical degree in Dublin. She remembers the year – her first as a student and away from home – very well.

Mother wrote to me regularly, but I'm afraid I didn't write to her much. It was all very exciting; I had met my future husband, and made lots of new friends, and life was just too full to think of home. At Christmas she sent me a wonderful Christmas cake, and all the girls in the hostel loved it. They even used to wake me up to beg for a slice of Mother's cake. I don't think I ever told her that. I have been very conscious of her influence in my adult life, though, in my faith, in the high standards she gave all her children and in the way I have raised my children.

Ana's mother died in childbirth, giving birth to her ninth child. Ana blamed her father and his sexuality and male pride for her mother's death. When he had been ill in hospital, her mother had run his large and complex business successfully on her own, and this had damaged his pride. He believed that his male standing in the community had been damaged by the evidence that his wife was as competent to run his business as he was. He decided that the only way to assert himself was for his wife to become pregnant, despite medical warnings that this could be dangerous for her. Out of her understanding and love, his wife agreed to take the risk. The result was, as the doctors had warned, her early death. For Ana, this was sufficient to make her reject her father entirely for many decades. The sexual relationship between her parents became to her, when she was only eighteen, an entirely negative and destructive force which had destroyed her mother.

Ana has the certainty that her mother supported her in her career. She went away for her medical training with her mother's blessing and pride, and she knows that her mother would have delighted in her success. She is sad that her mother and husband never met. 'My husband asked me if she would have liked him, and would she have approved of him? I told him I was sure she would. He has made me happy, and that would have been the most important thing for her. But also he is a devout Catholic, and she would have been so happy about that. All the rest – his successful career and all that has happened to us and our children, ofcourse she didn't see. I know she would have been a part of that, and I would like to believe that somewhere she knows, and is pleased about it all.'

Simone, throughout her Scottish childhood, was always close to her mother. Although she too has been divorced, this was not until after her mother's death. She has a clear sense of her mother's enjoyment of work outside the home, and the strong feeling that her mother had 'returned to herself' when she was able to go back to her nursing career after Simone's father died. Simone therefore feels confident in her mother's approval of her academic and career success.

She was very proud of me. She bragged to the whole village about 'her lassie'. I was the first of my family ever to leave Scotland. The village had supported me in getting a scholarship to University from the National Union of Mineworkers. I qualified because my mother's seven brothers were all miners.

Those seven brothers interfered a lot in my Mum's life, and I resisted that, with her support. They all married beautiful young women, who soon after their marriage became suddenly old and worn. I watched that happen, and vowed that I would not live that life. When they argued with her about me, she would say to them, 'She's intelligent enough to know what she's doing'. She never said that about herself, though, even though it was true.

Simone reflects on how much she absorbed from her mother about relationships with men, about marriage and babies, and all the female things which had been her mother's nursing career.

After I left home, I realised that she had taken a lover after Dad died. He was very handsome, but we all hated him because he was a policeman and so 'one of them' in our terms. I didn't like him, and so I never talked to her about him. Mum and I never really talked about sex. She used to tell us about her life during the Second World War, before her marriage, and I was fascinated by details like how she had made facials from egg-whites. She had a boy friend called Zigmund, a Polish soldier, and when she talked about him her eyes lit up. Still, as a young girl growing up I always felt 'outside the door' of my mother's room and what went on with all the other women.

I phoned her one day and said 'Guess what? I just got married!' She just said 'Who the hell to?' I don't know why I didn't tell her about my wedding. In some way I think I felt that I was being unfaithful to her. I couldn't tell her someone else had my heart. I had never learned that I could love other people without loving her less.

She was very proud of my beautiful house and my rich husband, and she loved to come to stay with us. She got on very well with my husband, and she wanted to look after us. She would brag about my life to the village when she got back – Her lassie was educated, cultured and rich!

When she came to stay with me after my marriage, she just wanted to clean for us – she even polished the light switches. I realised she just didn't feel at home with our friends, so I had to leave them to be with her. She was proud of my career, and loved to tell everyone back home in the village about what I was doing, but she couldn't really take part in it or understand it.

After my marriage I wondered about whether to have babies. I always thought that she would come and bring the baby up while I got on with my career. My daughter was born long after she died, and I found myself thinking so much of her. I loved breast-feeding my daughter, and I realised my mother had never had that with me because I was a tiny premature baby in an incubator. I felt I met my mother again when I became a mother.

Simone's reflections on sexuality however also contain a strongly negative element. 'I often think of the generations of women before me. My grandfather was a patriarch, and my grandmother was the Jewish girl abandoned by her family.' Simone's voice falters with emotion as she continues, 'When I graduated at twenty, Granny said to me, "I had five children when I was your age''. These women passed on to me a dowry of damage. They knew that people did things because of sexuality which damage families. It was that sexuality I couldn't face in my own adult life, just as I couldn't face too much love'.

There are strong echoes of Vivian Gornick's account of women's lives in her New York tenement in this story that Simone tells. Just as Vivian was to learn how much of her adult feelings about sex stemmed from the half-understood words and muttered conversations of her mother's women neighbours, so Simone felt that a 'dowry of damage' was passed down to her by the women of her family, and the half-understood conversations she overheard as a young girl between her mother and the women of her Scottish village. Only later did she piece together what she had seen and heard to understand the same story of damage, abuse, desire and need which determined so many of the women's attitudes towards their men in both the New York tenement and the Scottish mining village. In many neighbourhoods where poverty and prejudice still dominate today, there can be a world of negative learning passed on from one generation of women to another.

Jinny was fortunate in that she was able to share an understanding and appreciation of her educational work with her mother.

When I was a School Head, I always went into school on Sunday afternoons, to get things ready for the week ahead. Mummy loved to come with me to help. It was a very happy time of working together, and she really understood what I was doing. Once she said to me 'I'd like to have done this'. I realised just how much she had sacrificed in her life, without any complaint. She just always wanted the best for me, and supported me without question in my career. She was so proud of everything I did; I think I fulfilled all her hopes.

Jinny enjoyed an open relationship with her mother, and as we have seen earlier, they talked about sex openly. Jinny's mother replied directly and honestly to her daughter's questions, even about lesbianism which was then a taboo subject to many of her generation. Her gentle nudging of her daughter to understand the meaning of her young admirer's kiss is a charming demonstration of a good and wise mother dealing with her daughter's surprising youthful prudery.

Jinny now recalls with deep emotion one special moment with her mother on her wedding day, so poignantly reflecting the deep and special love between mother and daughter.

She was determined that my wedding dress was the best that could be found. She took me to the most expensive shop in town to choose it. On my wedding day, as I was leaving for the church she noticed that my bra-strap was showing and came to pin it back for me. As she did so, she pricked her finger and a tiny drop of blood went on the dress. She was dreadfully upset and said, 'I wanted your wedding to be perfect, and now the last thing I do for you is spoil your dress'. I was so sorry for her, as she had worked so hard to make it perfect for me, and of course it didn't matter.

Mummy was with me, in the room, when my son was born. She loved children and wished she'd had more than two. She was tremendously fond of my daughter, and they went on holiday together sometimes. She was always just there, as part of my adult life, in my job and family, just as she had been all my life as I grew up.

As the wife of an international businessman, Poppy spent much of her married life abroad, and so saw less of her mother than she would have liked. She did, however have what she calls 'nine wonderful years' with her mother after her father died. She had always resented her mother's loyalty and total attachment to Poppy's father – sometimes at the expense of time with her children at critical times of their lives. Poppy reflects how she has at times repeated this pattern of behaviour. 'When my daughter was doing her finals at university I stayed in South Africa with my husband instead of being with her in England. I just left her to cope on her own most of that period, even though I brought her out to see us.'

Poppy's mother made a career out of her marriage and mother-hood, and Poppy feels (contrary to the evidence of her active and successful counselling role) that she has done the same. 'I've never really done anything in my own right, although I have had

71

my ''sidelines''. I was a nurse before my marriage, and I have taught English as a foreign language. Later I trained as a counsellor and worked at that much more substantially. In that I suppose I am different from my mother.'

Poppy feels uncomfortable about the strong sexual undertones in her family relationships. She was worried when her father told her that her parents' sex life was unsatisfactory and that her mother was frigid. She felt that he was trying to have an intimacy with her which was inappropriate. The revelation about her mother made her worry whether she too would be frigid. Poppy also felt unhappy that it was her father, and not her mother, who told her about menstruation when she was a young girl. She comments dryly.

At my wedding it was the bride's father, not the bride's mother who cried all the way through.

Mummy didn't like my husband at first, neither did Daddy, but when they saw that he made me happy, and he became so successful in his career, they began to approve. I was very sad that Mummy also wasn't really nice to my daughters. She said what a pity it was that my eldest daughter didn't have eyes like mine. I know how much I bottled up about my childhood as an adult, because when I was forty I had a terrible row with my father when he was nasty to my younger daughter. All my bitterness about my own childhood came out. It was really very therapeutic for me, although probably it wasn't for him! Before that, I never had a good enough relationship with my father to talk to him about things that were important to me. I was determined that my daughters would have a good relationship with my husband.

After Daddy died, Mummy became totally dependent on her children. She came to live in our house, in a flat of her own. I was still in South Africa, but I came home every three months. It's sad, but I really felt good about our relationship when my father was no longer around. I think that's very indicative.

Helen feels that her choices in life have been made independently of any influence from her mother – and often in contradiction of her wishes. There is a wistfulness in her voice as she talks of her mother's response to the life she chose – a longing to believe that she was not a disappointment to her mother.

Mummy didn't want me to be a doctor. She had always wanted me to be an accountant. I never really knew how she felt about my career, although after she died my aunt, her sister, told me how proud of me Mummy had always been. She said Mummy 'idolised' me. She never showed any pride in my achievements to me, or seemed to care what I was doing in my career.

Her marriage to my stepfather was so happy. I always knew that their sex-life was strong and good. I thought of their bed as 'the happy bed'. All her life was devoted to making her second marriage work. She wanted me to marry well and have children. She didn't want me to marry my husband. He was twelve years older than me, and he wasn't a Jew. Although she thought well enough of him as a person, I don't think she ever reconciled herself to my marriage.

After we were engaged, I had a horrid letter from my aunt saying how evil it was to marry outside the faith. Mummy rang her up to defend me, and really told her off! She told her that I was already married in a registry office, so she'd better shut up. None of them knows to this day that I was married in church. Mummy came to the wedding, but she was terribly upset that I was married in a church. One of the worst things was that I disappointed her so much by having no children. She said to me once that I had taken away her chance of immortality: that was painful.

Our Jewish identity was very central to us, although neither of us was outwardly religious. I feel Jewish, and so did she. We both felt that this was not from choice – there was just no alternative.

Without bitterness, and with a rueful smile, Helen adds, 'After all, no one would choose to be a Jew'.

Jane too describes an 'ambivalent' relationship with her mother, from their early days travelling from India to Hong Kong and back to India again. Nevertheless, she is grateful for the support she received in her career.

All my memories of her are of a working, busy mother, so there was never any question of whether I would have a career. In the autobiography which she left, Mummy tells how before she became pregnant with me she had a vision that there would be a child (that was me and indeed my younger sister) and a death (and that was my brother). It was a remarkable vision, because she had been told she couldn't have any more children after my brother was born. When she was pregnant with me, a fortune-teller told her that the child would be famous. When I was born, though, I was a girl, so Mummy decided I couldn't be the one who was famous. Later, after my sister was born, she decided it was me, and she thought I should be Foreign Secretary!

While I was an undergraduate at Cambridge Mummy was running a hotel to support the three of us. She had to live with a lot of snobbery in a small village, and I admired her enormously for the way she coped with all that. I liked to help her in my vacations, because she so needed support. After I graduated, she was able to give up the hotel and she and I lived together. I was teaching then, and this was a real disappointment to her. I always felt I was a disappointment to her. I wish she had lived to see that when I found my real career, working in the field of development, I did conduct research which became famous in its field.

She liked my husband very much, and in fact she disapproved of my work in development consultancy and research because it involved my leaving him so often.

When we first lived abroad she used to spend time with us every year, and when the children were little she enjoyed them. They loved her as their grandmother. When she was in her fifties she had developed a deep faith, and I think that was important to her in that period of her life.

In spite of her sexual ignorance at the beginning of the marriage, she seems to have been very happy in the marriage while it lasted. I always felt that she was really still in love with my father, long after the marriage was over. Her autobiography never really criticises him, or has a bad word for the way he treated her. Even at the end of his life she wrote to him and said she wanted to take care of him in his last illness, after all, she was a nurse; but he sent her letter on to me saying, 'Your mother is writing threatening letters to me. Please tell her to stop.' It was such a cruel end to their relationship.

Chapter Six
Time of Parting

It's time to carry her out.
I hear a childish voice – though not a child's–
Screaming *No, No,*

You can't take her
You're not allowed
You can't take my mother.
from Wanda Barford, 'The Last Fitting'

Wanda Barford writes in her beautiful poem about the moment when the undertaker's men came to carry her mother's body from the room where, a little while earlier, Wanda had found her dead. Her shout of almost primitive pain, 'No, No . . . You can't take my mother' resonates with so many women as they recall the disbelief, denial, and wrenching pain of that moment of physical parting.

No daughter is immune. On our television screens in 2002, many of us saw the look of frozen grief on the face of Queen Elizabeth II as she watched her 'beloved' mother's coffin borne into Westminster Hall. That look resonated with every bereaved daughter's sense of numbness and emptiness when, no matter how expected the end, or how long the life has been, their mother's physical presence is lost to them.

None of the women in these stories found it easy to talk about the time of their mother's last days. For me, the period both before and after my mother's death seem permanently frozen in time, like nothing else that had ever happened before or since. I was not with her when she died – and how painful that was to me – but I know that she had said her goodbye to me when I visited her the day before. Although she seemed past knowing what was happening, or who I was, I sat holding her hand and spoke to her from time to time, bending down close to her ear in the hope that she could, somehow, hear and recognise my voice. After a long time, I bent down once more to her and said, 'Mummy dear, it's Pauline. I have to go now'. Like a miracle, she lifted her head from the pillow, focused her eyes on my face, and with tremendous effort, gave me the sweetest, dearest smile before sinking again into what seemed unconsciousness. That memory is infinitely precious to me, as her last and most loving gift.

Not one of the women I interviewed had managed to be with her mother at the moment of her death, although some were able to take care of their mothers in the last days of life. Others looked for ways to give them special recognition and love in the rituals which followed their death. Some were travelling and away from their mothers at the last hour; others had been there until just an hour or two before. Hospice personnel, who are such gentle experts in death, teach us that people often choose to die when their closest loved ones have gone out of the room. Perhaps the pain of leaving those most dear to us is easier when they are no longer physically present.

The opportunity to care for our mother in her last weeks and months is a unique return for the years of our childhood when she took care of us. Kate Millett has written an extraordinary brave story of the way she cared for her dying mother in her powerful book *Mother Millett*. Unwilling at first to face up to the sacrifice of her own life and relationships if she were to take on the care of her mother, she nevertheless found she simply could not bear to see her mother confined to the quality of life which a nursing home offered, with its lack of life and colour and above all of personal dignity and freedom. She visited her mother in the nursing home her sister had chosen, intending just to satisfy herself that all was well. Instead, she found the heart-achingly 'helpless little figure' who was her mother waiting with her clothes on and bag packed, with a complete and childlike faith that she would be 'rescued' by her daughter Kate.

Millett did indeed rescue her mother, and took her home for what at first was going to be just a few nights. Eventually Kate recognised her mother's deep need to live her life, however limited, in her own home and with the familiar possessions and people around her. Not without some grave misgivings, Kate bravely decided to give up a large portion of her life to her mother's care, abandoning friends, conference engagements, work and sources of income to perform what she saw first as a labour of duty, and then as a labour of love.

It was not easy. With ruthless self-knowledge, Millett tells us all her guilt; her wounding of her mother with snobbery, or humiliating her in front of her friends by taking her to dinner in a wheel-chair. But she tells us also of the slow build up of understanding; of the love which carries them through the most difficult and exhausting moments; of Kate's battle with the medical profession, bureaucracies, social workers and an appalling professional lack of humanity. Even her own sister had scant understanding or sympathy with what she was doing.

Kate has no doubt that what she did is right. She succeeded in giving her mother two final years of dignity; the right to spend them in her own home, with all the aids and care her daughter's determination had won for her. In caring for her mother, Kate found that she was caring for herself, restoring some of her lost childhood, and rediscovering the love which bound her through life and beyond to her mother.

In literature there are many stories of daughters who care for and give comfort to their dying mothers – and so to themselves – as well as stories of the painful last goodbye. The story told by Campbell Armstrong in his book *All that Really Matters* of his ex-wife Eileen and her daughter Barbara describes poignantly, sometimes using words from Barbara's own journal, the final parting between two women who had been separated for over forty years, only to find each other as both were dying.

Eileen had carried the scar of her Caesarean section for forty-two years, all that remained, so she believed, of the daughter she had lost. When they were at last reunited, Eileen was able to show Barbara that scar. For Barbara, it was an awesome and overwhelmingly joyous moment to find the place where she had emerged from her mother's womb, the evidence of the end to her search. That physical mark of her birth was to become to Barbara an affirmation of her identity. However happy she had been with her adoptive parents, her joy at finding the mother of her birth was complete.

Barbara was able to travel to the United States to visit her mother on only three occasions; once immediately after the phone call had first put them in touch, once at Christmas time, just a few months before her mother died, and finally, to be with her when she died. The two very ill women had a lifetime to catch up in a few days of endless talk and hugs, caring and inspiring each other to fight the cancer that had attacked them both. As a nurse, Barbara was able to give practical help and comfort to her dying mother, and the closeness and love between them seemed as if the years of separation had never been. Small but happy mother-daughter moments, like those recalled with happiness by so many of the women who speak to us in these memories – Barbara combing her mother's hair and trying out new hairstyles – were infinitely precious, because they had come only at the end of both their lives.

On the second visit, the mother and daughter vowed to fight against the cancer together, gave each other strength and even hope, and shared their memories and stories of the years apart. Although she would have chosen to spend just one Christmas with her mother, out of the forty-two they had spent apart, Barbara knew the time had come to say goodbye. She returned to her husband and family in England wondering if she would ever see her mother again.

When Eileen's friend told her that the end was near, however, and despite her own weakness and increasing poor health, not to mention the financial burden of travel from England to Arizona, Barbara made one last visit. Eileen was slipping away, but managed to pull herself up to hug her daughter as she entered the bedroom. With the words, 'I love you, Barbara, I've missed you', she settled down in her daughter's embrace and curled up to sleep. For several days, with Eileen's three sons, her exhusband and her close friend, Barbara stayed near her all the time. At the end, Barbara had only a few moments alone with the mother she had lost at birth, and found near death. She wrote in her journal that she had lain down beside her mother, gently and with infinite love rested her head against her, and sung to her Eileen's favourite song 'The Rose'. She kissed her then, knowing it was for the last time, and said goodbye.

A year later, when she herself died, a photograph of the mother she had known for only four short, but intensely precious months, was beside her bed.

The need to care and give comfort to a dying mother is a theme of some of the stories our women tell. As a trained nurse, Poppy was able to look after her mother in the last months of her life. Her mother had lived in a separate apartment in Poppy's home for some years before she died, and although Poppy and her husband were living abroad for five of those years, they were back together for the last eighteen months, which Poppy calls 'wonderful months. She was always just next door, so I could pop in to chat to her. We would go shopping together, have pub lunches, a real mother-daughter period. She was quite a mate in a way.'

Poppy recalls when, as her mother's health worsened, she was one day rushed into hospital in considerable pain. 'The Doctor on duty asked me if I wanted him to try to resuscitate, if her heart should stop. I said "ask her" and so he did. Mummy said, "I want to see the Millennium in", so that was that. She came home again, but she had had a colostomy. While she was in hospital I visited her every day, and noticed that she had developed bedsores. She then had circulation problems in her leg.'

Poppy cried as she relived the period of her mother's illness and pain.

After she came home, she had good care. The morphine she was on made her aggressive. That was so sad, because it was so unlike her true self. I used to bully her to get up and walk about, but she got horrid sores and gangrene, and had to go back into hospital, now really very ill. I stayed overnight with her, and to my amazement she started speaking Swedish to me. She hadn't done that since I was a baby.

Finally I insisted on bringing her back home again. She was finding it hard to die, and kept asking me to give her the 'big shot', but I said 'of course I won't do that'. I worried about her all the time. I used to walk down the hall and peep through the keyhole to see that she was still safe in bed.

The day before she died I went to church. A man fainted in the middle of the service, and because I am a nurse, I had to go to help. Afterwards the vicar came over to thank me, and asked about my mother. When I told him how ill she was, he offered to come to see her.

His visit was splendid. Mummy was absolutely her most charming self. She said she wasn't worried about me, but she did worry about her son. Anyway, he offered Communion, and she and I had it together. I cried all the way through. That night, the nurse and I sat talking beside her, and I was peeling apples as we talked. I said goodnight to her and went to bed late, but at three in the morning the nurse came to call me. When I got there, she had died just a few minutes earlier. I do so wish I had been there. I still think of that night so often, and think that I should have been.

Although the memory of her mother's suffering is painful, Poppy has the comfort of knowing that she was able to ease her mother's dying by her care and the comfort of her presence and her love. The wonderful last day is a healing memory of the rightness of the Communion ritual, the grace of her mother's charm, and the blessed ordinariness of the quiet hours of domestic chores at her mother's bedside. Perhaps Poppy's mother too had said her private goodbye earlier, in the comfort of the shared Communion and the quiet evening of three women sitting together with the apples and their talk.

Helen also regrets that she missed the moment of her mother's death. As a doctor, she felt a need to be able to care for her mother in her last illness, but the great geographical distance between them and the demands of her career made this difficult.

Mummy was diagnosed with breast cancer eight years before she died. She and my stepfather were in Holland and I went over to collect them and bring her back to England for treatment. She had a mastectomy and was very ill and weak afterwards. She kept fainting, I think largely from the mental and physical shock. She did recover, though, and in fact it was my stepfather who died first, four years later. Mummy had always wanted to go to Australia, as her brothers and sister were there, and now Father had died, she felt she could become Jewish with her family again. She went for a visit and then decided that she would move permanently to Australia. She was seventy-two, the same age as her mother had been when the rest of the family moved there.

She bought a nice house in Melbourne and I went to visit her after she had settled in. She was well, just fine and happy. A few months later, though, the cancer returned and she was very ill. I went to see her, and stayed for a few weeks to look after her. It was obvious that she wasn't going to be able to look after herself, so we looked for a good care home for her, and she moved in just before Christmas, while I was still there. I spent Christmas with her, and the home was very nice, but I had to return to the UK, as I had a job interview coming up. I got the job, just what I had wanted, and my employers were very understanding about my mother. She got steadily worse, and so they told me I could take as long as I needed to go and be with her. I went back to Australia and spent seven weeks with her. I wanted to take care of her. I rented a two-bedroom apartment and hired a car so she could come and stay with me, and we could drive around together. It didn't work. She only stayed two nights, and then said she wanted to be back in the Home. I took her out every day, and we did do things together.

Helen's memories of the last days of that visit are still painful.

Mummy was so ill. She was like a little bird sitting in the Home waiting for me each day. I remember one time when I took her to the beach; she was so weak she could hardly get up from sitting on the blanket in the sunshine.

In the end, I had to go back. It was heartbreaking to leave her. She saw me off from the forecourt of the Home wearing a beautiful blue dress she had made herself. Even then, we neither of us could say all the things we wanted to say, we had to make it a sort of joking thing. I said to her 'You have been a very good little Mummy to me', and she said, 'You've

been a very good daughter'. That was the last time I spoke
to her. I drove off, leaving her standing there alone on the
forecourt.

Helen returned home sadly, reflecting that her mother's assurance that she had been a 'good daughter' was not deserved. 'I
don't feel I was good to her. I think if I'd asked her to come
and live with me after Father died, instead of going to Australia,
she would have been pleased; she wanted me to say it. Even
after my visit, she got very confused and wrote letters saying she
wanted to come back home. But I knew that she and I could
never share a kitchen.'

In April of that year, soon after Helen had returned to her
medical work, her uncle called her urgently back to Australia.

I took a plane straight away, but the journey seemed endless.
We had to stop in Brisbane en route, and I was very distressed.
As we waited in Brisbane airport I saw the Archbishop of
Canterbury and Terry Waite who were travelling on the same
plane. Even though I'm not a Christian I had a sudden urge
to go and ask him for a prayer, but I didn't dare disturb him.

I arrived off the plane in the morning of the day she died.
I went straight to the hospital, but she wasn't conscious. I
think, though, she knew I was there, because her breathing
changed, it stilled for a moment when I spoke to her. My uncle
took me back to his home to rest, as I'd been travelling for
two days and I was exhausted, but I couldn't settle away from
her, so I went back to see her at lunchtime. This time she
didn't react at all to my presence, and eventually I did go back
to my uncle's house to rest. At eight in the evening, the phone
call came from the hospital to say she had died.

My uncle and I drove straight over to the hospital and went
in to see her. Even from an hour or two before, she had changed
so. In death she looked so peaceful and much younger. My
uncle said, 'I've got my little sister back again.' I do so wish
I had been there with her to the very end.

Helen's mother seems to have waited to know at a level
deep within her consciousness that her much-loved daughter

83

was there, before passing quietly away with no need for more
sad goodbyes.

Jinny's story of the last contact with her mother has many
similar features. Abroad on educational business, she also had to
travel in haste to be with her dying mother. In the last year or
two of her life, her mother had become blind and unable to look
after herself. After living in a granny flat in Jinny's home for
seven years, her blindness became such a handicap that she
needed constant care. Jinny still feels some discomfort that her
mother moved into a home for the blind, not least because she
remembers the selfless devotion to her grandmother which her
mother had shown for twenty years.

> I deeply regret putting her in a home, but it would otherwise
> have meant my giving up my job, and I knew she wouldn't
> have wanted that. She became forgetful and confused towards
> the end.
>
> I was working in California when the call came from my
> brother to say Mummy was failing very fast, so I should come
> back quickly. I took the next plane, and even after landing at
> Heathrow, it took hours to get to her. She was in a coma, and
> so I wasn't able to talk to her, but I know she realised I'd
> come, because when I held her hand and spoke, she squeezed
> my hand back. I was jet-lagged and very tired, so my brother
> took me home, but they phoned and said she was slipping
> away and we should come back. We went straight away, but
> we were too late. I so wish I'd stayed with her.

Like Helen's mother, Jinny's mother seems to have waited just
to know that her beloved daughter had come. Having said her
silent goodbye, she could die in peace.

In their busy lives, many of the women were on the move
when the call came to summon them to their mother's bedside.
Jane was in Italy at a conference when someone came in to say
that there was a message for her. She left the conference room,
and when she got outside, the messenger had to tell her that her
mother was dead. The memory of the events of those days is
infinitely painful for her, and she had to stop speaking to deal
with her distress several times as she spoke.

Mummy had been in a home for some time. She couldn't look after herself any more, and so my sister had to choose a place for her. I was away living and working in Germany, so I didn't have any part in the choice. She had been pleased enough with the home in the first year, but then she became depressed and physically weak. I wish I'd seen her more, but it was difficult to get back from Germany. Even when I came home for a week I only saw her once or twice. She was so tired, and seemed glad to give up. When I visited her she did know who I was, and was glad to see me, but it was difficult to get any conversation going, as she just talked about her immediate discomforts. To me it was particularly sad that she seemed to have lost her faith. When she was younger she had a deep faith, but in the last years she never mentioned her faith, or derived any comfort from it.

Jane was not able to be with her mother or have any formal exchange of final words, as her mother was already dead when the news reached her.

When the news came that she had died, I hurried to get a train to Rome so that I could catch a plane back to the UK. I had a carriage to myself, and just sobbed all the way. We had never said any proper goodbye; it was three months since I had even seen her, and there were so many bits and pieces of unfinished business between us. I just wanted to know that she was at peace. I thought of how she had been when she was younger and my children were little. She had come to visit us every year and stayed wherever we were around the world. I didn't even see her when I got back to England; the undertaker had already taken over.

Simone too found it difficult to speak of the events of her mother's death.

After my marriage, mother came from Scotland to stay with us often; she liked my husband. One New Year I noticed she was very quiet, and I caught her weeping. She wouldn't say why, but when she came down at Easter I was worried that she just wasn't herself. One night I climbed into bed beside her and asked her to tell me what was the matter. She told me she had a lump in her shoulder. It was Easter and I couldn't get the local GP to see her, and I was frantic. We went to a dinner party with some friends and I burst into tears at the table. When I told them what was the matter, they helped immediately and organised for her to see a consultant and get an X-ray at the hospital. The hospital found a massive lung cancer.

I organised a programme of radiotherapy treatment for her in London, so she could be with us, but she said she would have to go back up to Scotland first, to close up her house there. She went off for a few days, and we went to our cottage in Wales to try to come to terms with the shock and think through all I planned to do to get her better. I walked the fields alone with a notebook, listing all the stuff I wanted to talk to her about. There seemed so much to say, to explain and to understand. She mustn't leave me yet. When we returned to our London house, the police were waiting for me, and they told me she had died.

We went straight up to Scotland, but when we got there, it was awful. The windows were hung with sheets for the death, as we do in Scotland, and the house was full of people. She was in a room by herself in her coffin, and I just walked past everyone to go and be with her. I talked to her for ages, angrily telling her off for not waiting for me, asking her all the things I still needed to ask her. I told her 'I was going to make you better, don't you understand?' I don't think I was quite sane.

Later, I realised that going off like that to die was just the most loving thing she could have done. She and I had always been faithful to each other; she had my heart, as I had hers. There was no way she and I could ever have said goodbye.

A. feels great sorrow at the difficult period her mother suffered towards the end of her life.

When Mummy was visiting us in England I took her to a specialist in London and he put her on a new form of insulin for her diabetes. He didn't explain to us how important it was to get the timing of the injections right, and one day she collapsed because her blood sugar level had gone so low. I went to wake her up that afternoon, and she was in a diabetic coma. I didn't know what to do so I phoned my husband and he said 'get an ambulance'. The ambulance took her to hospital, and she recovered.

After she went back to India she was never really well, but she survived for several years, and I went to visit her often. At the end of her life, in her last illness, she kept saying 'Where's my daughter?' The nurse told her I was far away in England, but my brother phoned me and said she was asking for me. He asked her directly if she wanted me to come, and she said, 'Yes'. My daughter and I travelled at once to see her.

That time together was really nice. She perked up when I came, and we had lots of nice long talks together. I used to lie on her bed beside her, and we talked about so many things. It was the first time we had talked about my divorce. When it was happening, she never said a word. I found out that she did understand, and she loved me, but it had made her very, very sad. Eventually I had to come back to England, and one week later my brother telephoned me to say she had died.

It was terrible, unbelievable. I wasn't there. The pain was unbelievable. It was all happening in Bombay and I was here. There was nothing I could do, so I just sat by myself and read the prayers for the dead.

A. still feels that the good visit she had with her mother was perhaps all her mother had waited for, and that, after it, she was ready to go in peace.

Peggy's mother had a protracted period of poor health in her later years. She had a stroke while in her fifties and had high blood pressure. Peggy remembers the hard time her mother had.

She put on a lot of weight and had to drive instead of walk, although the doctor had told her to get out and about. When Dad was in hospital she walked to see him every day and then she did lose weight. But later she had dizzy turns and became confused. She'd leave food burning on the stove while she watched television. My sister and I tried to get her to have home help but it was very difficult because she just sent them away! She was very independent. She also refused to come and live with us, although after Dad died in November my sister and I brought her down to London for what she insisted was a short time.

She spent Christmas with me, and then went on to my sister after Christmas. She was taken ill there, and had to go into hospital. They only kept her for a few days and sent her back to my sister's home. My niece thought she'd had a stroke, but the hospital said no. The day after she came back, my sister went out to work and phoned her later on to see if she was all right. When she got no answer, she rushed home and found Mummy lying unconscious on the kitchen floor.

She was taken in to hospital, but was pronounced dead. My sister got a message through to me, but just to say that Mummy was back in hospital and would I please come, but no hurry. As I drove to the hospital, I thought 'She's dead' – I don't know why, but I felt it. When I arrived at the hospital it was awful. She wasn't in the ward and I had to join a queue at Reception just to find out what had happened. The receptionist was horrid. She made no attempt to break the news gently, or to offer me any sympathy or privacy. I didn't see her until she was in the funeral home.

The death of Ana's mother in Zanzibar came as a terrible blow to her young daughter then far away in Ireland. Ana was a very young medical student, living in a Catholic hostel for women students, when the news came that her mother had died giving birth to her ninth child. Ana was only eighteen, and her mother was only forty, and Ana had never even considered the possibility of losing her mother.

One day the nuns in the hostel came to see me and told me that Mother was seriously ill. I was very worried as to what that meant. That night I had a dream that she had died. The next day the head nun came to see me, and took me aside into a small room. She told me then that Mother had died. I met my boyfriend later that day, and I just couldn't stop sobbing.

He didn't know what to do, so he took me to see his mother, so that she could comfort me. It wasn't really possible for anyone to help, though; it was my experience not anyone else's.

I got a letter from home after a few days, telling me all the details. I was allowed to go back to Africa for a few months after I had finished my exams. I got there two months after she died, but I found that she had already started to prepare for my home-coming before she died. She had made lots of my favourite sweets and things, and it was so terribly sad to see them, and to think of how she had looked forward to my coming.

I couldn't have known when I said goodbye to her at the age of seventeen to go off to Ireland that it was the last time I would see her. She had cooked me a lovely big breakfast that morning, and we said goodbye. I never saw her again. Although I was told that hundreds of people turned up for the funeral, I wasn't there, and I missed all that. I felt I had never buried her.

Judith's mother lived for only a year after her husband's death. True to all she had told her children about their deep and loving relationship, she seemed to lose the will to live without him. She was only five stones (seventy pounds) in weight when she died.

Judith speaks about the last months of her mother's life with an understanding which came to her late in their relationship.

In her last years she gained my respect, both for her care for my father and for her own fastidiousness. She was always immaculately dressed. When she was dying she asked my son to go and see her. She told him, 'I'm not going to be glamorous any more, and I don't want you to remember me like that. Please don't come to see me again. Just speak to me sometimes on the phone.' It was brave of her and quite typical.

Judith was very unhappy, frequently breaking down in tears even in the company of friends in the period before her mother's death. She simply could not imagine life without her mother

89

there. 'I said to her ''What about me? You're going to leave me on my own'' but she just said ''Don't be silly – I'll be there. I'll be the first star you see at night''.

'I was with her half an hour before she died. I said goodbye to her and drove back to London. By the time I reached home there was a message waiting for me to say that she had died. I felt like an orphan.'

Anne's story of her mother's death gives her intense pain. She was working happily on her anthropological research and was totally unprepared for the news. 'It still seems impossible to believe that someone can appear to be normal and well in the evening, yet dead the next morning.'

Anne's mother had been exhibiting symptoms of hardening of the arteries and shortness of breath for some time. Although her family had no recognition of the seriousness of their mother's ill health, Anne now believes that her mother already knew that she was fatally ill and perhaps had only a very short time to live. She bases this belief on her mother's behaviour in the last few months of her life.

A month or two before she died, I took my parents to the Isle of Wight for them to choose a house which I was going to buy for them. We stayed in a very nice hotel, which had a musician to play in the dining room in the evenings. I arranged that as we went into dinner each night, the musician played their special song 'The Thought of You'. They had been childhood sweethearts, and the song was from the Second World War. She was thrilled with that, and it seemed to make them both very happy. We found an ideal house, and my father was very enthusiastic about it. She however seemed detached, and I wonder now if she knew that she wouldn't live to be there. In fact, she died before the contracts were exchanged. She had always said to us 'Do you know what makes God laugh? Plans!' She taught me that no matter how carefully you plan, events can just blow all your plans apart. She was certainly right about that in this case.

One incident torments Anne even eighteen months after her mother's death.

Some time earlier I had saved up some money to buy Mother
a necklace of real matched pearls. She loved them and wore
them all the time. She wouldn't even lend them to me, in case
I broke them, and in a way that pleased me because it showed
how much they meant to her. Two months before she died,
we were sitting together in front of the window and she suddenly took off the pearls and said, 'Here you are – have the
pearls'. She had already given me most of her other jewellery,
but I didn't want to take them, as it just felt wrong to me, and
we started to have quite an argument about it. We'd never
really argued before, but I screamed at her, and shocked my
father at the vehemence of my reaction. She said she didn't
want any more things bought for her, and that made me really
angry.

Anne can't now believe that she shouted at her mother and
became almost hysterical about such an issue. It is, however,
apparent that Anne's mother understood that the pearls were not
the real issue. They were only the outward symbol of what each
was trying to say. 'After I had shouted at her that I wouldn't
take the pearls, Mother said to me, "You can't face the thought
of me dying, can you?" At the end of the evening, she once
again insisted that I take the pearls, and I felt I couldn't argue
any more, so I took them away.'

The poignancy of this dialogue between mother and daughter
is that they were unable to talk about death and parting. Perhaps
Anne's mother wanted to bring the issue out into the open, but
Anne was refusing to see the evidence of her mother's failing
health. She now feels regret that she wanted to keep up the
pretence that all was well, blindly ignoring all her mother's
attempts to manage her affairs in her own way, and pass on her
most precious possession to her daughter in her lifetime, not after
her death.

Anne admits that she was in denial about her mother's state
of health. She talks of the last day of her mother's life, and is
overcome with the still raw grief of the memory.

On the day she died, my son was staying with her and my
father, and he took her out shopping at my suggestion. I told

him to buy her some new things; I wanted her to have new things 'to keep her'. He bought her a dress and a handbag and she bought herself some new make-up. She and my father and son had a lovely day together, and they sat talking by the fire after dinner until she went to bed about half past eleven. She had two glasses of wine and was very relaxed and happy.

My father woke up at eight the next morning to make them a cup of tea as he did every day. She was dead in the bed beside him. He ran to wake my son to come and help – I don't think he wanted to believe that she was actually dead. My twenty-seven-year-old son said, 'Don't worry; I'm trained in first aid'. He tried to give her mouth-to-mouth resuscitation, but she had been dead for four hours and rigor mortis had set in. My son had never seen anyone dead before, so I don't think he realised. He has suffered from severe depression since, especially as my father kept asking him if he was sure she was dead. He was given too much responsibility, and now he feels to blame in some way.

My son called me, but when I answered he put the phone down. He had to call back twice more before he could bring himself to say 'Gran's dead'. I was in such shock when he told me that I said, 'I'm on my way to Hartlepool', which was where they had lived, although they were then in Bristol; I had switched back in my shock. I travelled down to Bristol and took charge of all the arrangements for her funeral. I just couldn't believe it had happened. I felt as if my whole life and the whole family had fallen apart.

One of the leading experts in the psychology of the dying and the bereaved is Dr Dewi Rees. In his book *Death and Bereavement* he quotes a list of rights and entitlements of the dying which were first identified by a study group for the charity Age Concern. For those whose death is foreseen, and preceded by a period in which the end approaches, these include the right to retain control of what happens, to have time to say goodbye, and to be afforded dignity and privacy. In the accounts from the women interviewed here we can see how important these factors were for them as well as for their dying mothers. In different and entirely personal ways, each mother dealt with her own death and her daughter's grief, many with immense courage and love. Those who for various reasons could not ease their daughter's impending sense of loss, or who were unable or unwilling to speak of it, made the process of grieving harder.

Chapter Seven
The Comfort of Ritual

On my bookshelves I have a treasured book of photographs selected from the world's photographers, called *The Family of Woman*. Towards the end of this amazing and beautiful collection is a series of pictures from Italy which I find infinitely moving. The first shows the body of a very old woman lying on a large bed, while bending over her an elderly woman, one supposes her daughter, is gently closing her eyes. The two women are alone in the room. The next picture shows the body now laid out ready for burial, and the younger woman, her last work of caring complete, bends over to kiss the dead face. In the third photograph, she is sitting down beside the bed, bent forward and resting her head down on the covers beside the body, in a final posture perhaps of grief, or perhaps of private prayer and farewell. A pair of crutches – hers or her mother's? – is propped up beside her.

The pictures to me sum up the deep significance of the last duties and rituals which we perform for our mothers, woman to woman, when we can do no more for the living person. These rituals are as much for our sakes as for hers. In present western societies, we leave much of the formal ritual to the undertakers and funeral directors, but still look for our own personal ways of using the rites of the funeral, the disposal of possessions and the marking of the grave to show our respect for the dead and to heal our grieving.

There are still private and personal rituals, of meaning only to the bereaved and the loved one they mourn, which help and ease us through the time of loss. The poet Wanda Barford, whose collection of poems *A Moon at the Door* chart so vividly the story of a daughter loving, losing and grieving for her mother, writes of the way she waited with her mother's body for the funeral director, just as Poppy had done. Every bereaved daughter can identify with the story she tells in her poem 'Comforters'. As she waited for the men who would take her mother away, she sat beside her on the floor where her mother had fallen, knowing that it was the last time they would be alone together. She describes how, from when she was a little girl, her mother had rolled up handkerchiefs to tie and fold them into little mice for her. In her later years, her mother had made them for herself, and taken them to bed with her for comfort. Wanda gathered them up from the empty bed and wanting to do one last thing to give comfort, arranged them around her mother's body. It was a private ritual, the more meaningful because it was something shared and known to them both. The little mice had been a source of comfort to the daughter in childhood and then for the mother in her old age. They were now the daughter's gift of comfort to her mother in death.

The many after-death rituals which all societies have established serve both to give honour to the dead and to give comfort to the living. For as long as we can find evidence, these rituals have been bound up with religious belief and the need to give value to human life. The great early twentieth-century anthropologist Malinowski believed that death was the most important source of religion. While this may not be the view of all social scientists, it is certainly true that for many millions of people the promise of immortality which most religions offer, the defeat of death by life which continues after the death of the body, encourages the bereaved to turn towards religious services and rituals to help them bear the burden of their loss.

In 1979, the anthropologists R. Huntingdon and P. Metcalf published a fascinating book called *Celebrations of Death: The Anthropology of Mortuary Ritual*, in which they review the rituals observed by a wide range of different societies and communities. They make the point powerfully that although the rituals vary enormously, characterised more by their diversity than by uniformity, such responses to death are never random, but always 'meaningful and expressive' to the living community. They also emphasise that, within each community, the rituals of death change only very slowly, and the resistance to such change is great. Perhaps the furious reaction to Jessica Mitford's groundbreaking book *The American Way of Death*, which called for an end to the elaborate and expensive rituals which funeral directors were offering to the bereaved, was an example of such resistance to change. People did not want more simplified procedures, even when Mitford exposed how those who grieved were exploited by the funeral directors who served them.

The classic study of the meaning of funerary rites was that undertaken by the French sociologist Robert Hertz in 1907 – not translated into English until 1960. Hertz's studies led him to believe that the rites which societies follow in the face of death affirm two things: first, that death is lasting, for the experience of those remaining in this life, but also, that, for the person who has died, it is a transition. The key feature of the first, he believed, was that the living society reaffirmed its own continuity even in the face of the loss of one or more of its members, by mortuary rites in which 'the last word must remain with life'. At the same time, the rites confer a new identity to the departed, who enter into a new era, as members of the community of 'the ancestors' or 'the saints triumphant' or whatever identity the religion and beliefs of the mourners bestow on those who have left this life.

Hertz describes how many societies have a two-stage ritual, a 'double burial' for the final disposal of the body of the deceased. The belief is that death is only complete when both stages of the disposal of the body are completed. In the first, the flesh is destroyed, either by cremation or when the body has completely decomposed. In this first stage of burial or cremation, the identity of the dead as a member of the continuing society is removed. In the second stage, the bones or ashes are given a further ritual disposal, and it is at that point that the deceased is assigned a permanent new status and identity as one of the ancestors.

The importance of the second stage, Hertz observed, was that it closed 'the dark period' where death and grief, and the feeling of revulsion towards the rotting or burning corpse can cloud all thoughts of the departed. In the second rites, the dead person is assigned feelings of 'reverent confidence' and a new status as a member of the honoured community of the departed. Hertz observed, and other anthropologists have further developed his thesis, that in so establishing a separate society for the dead, the living community was regenerated or recreated.

Most poignantly, he believed that is why in so many ways this ritual gives to death the significance of rebirth. Death resembles birth, in that both are a renewal and a rite of passage from one status to another. There are overtones here of the humanist view of death as a sacrifice of the individual for the continuity of life for the human species.

Modern cremations, when followed by burial of the ashes, can offer the comfort of this 'two-stage' closing of the chapter of life on earth and opening up a new identity for the deceased. Jane found that the funeral of her mother brought her little comfort, but the later burial of her ashes beside her long-lost son, Jane's big brother, brought a time of peace and closure she had not felt before. Peggy too found that organising for her mother's ashes to be brought back to the North of England, her true home, and their burial there brought a sense of rightness to the arrangements. Anne was still waiting to decide what to do for her second stage of ritual, the burial of her mother's ashes, when I interviewed her. She did not yet feel ready for that final closure.

Virginia Ironside, in her book entitled sarcastically *You'll Get Over It*, says that British funerals in particular are designed to force us to face 'the mystery and horror' of death. She feels that funerals with the central role of the coffin or casket and the presence of the mourners at the graveside or crematorium 'ram home' the message of death – publicly acknowledging that a person is gone from society and their community.

One of the most powerful and beautiful rituals is in the Jewish Orthodox custom of 'Hevrah Kaddisha', which is a washing of the dead. Women wash women, and men wash men. In the book *How I Find Her* about her mother's death, which brings to us again the theme of a daughter 'finding' her mother, Genie Zeiger describes how she and her sister took part in this most beautiful ceremony for the washing of their mother's body.

Together with four other women of her mother's Jewish community, the sisters first join hands outside the funeral home and talk about their mother, her life, her achievements, her personality. They then go to the room where she is lying, and a prayer is said asking for God's help in performing the task of the washing. Then follows a direct speech to the woman whose body is to be washed: calling her by her name, they offer an apology for 'any indignity we may cause'. Another prayer follows, asking for angels of mercy to come to her.

The women then pour three pitchers of water on the mother's body, chanting afterwards 'Tahorah He' which means 'she is pure'. After a reading of some lovely verses from the Song of Solomon, the women slowly wrap the body in white linen, praying again at each stage of the dressing. A linen headdress is placed over her eyes, 'to protect her from the blinding light of God' and her head is rested on a pillow filled with earth from the land of Israel. Zeiger tells how she and her sister helped the other women to lift their mother's body into her shroud, and each kissed her before they left the room where she would stay until her burial.

A similar ceremony is found amongst followers of the Baha'i religion, an offshoot of the Muslim faith, which is now one of the fastest growing religions in Africa and South East Asia. Although not usually practised by followers of Baha'i in western countries, elsewhere the body is washed by a family member, with due ritual, and wrapped in five sheets of white silk or cotton to make a shroud. A special ring is placed on the finger and the body is then put into a coffin made of material as durable as the family can afford. This is because the body must be shown the respect due to something which once was the bearer of an immortal soul. Followers are taught that the interment must be conducted with 'radiance and serenity'.

For the Christian, death is the gateway into new life, a life amongst 'the saints triumphant' as some say, or a life of bliss in heaven. Catholics speak of a period in purgatory, through which the soul moves towards eternal peace and redemption. Many Christians today find it hard to believe in the concept of personal and eternal survival, choosing instead to envision some sort of impersonal but eternal union with God. For Christians it is essential to believe that something – the soul, the essence, of the person who dies – is preserved beyond death, and is accepted into the loving hands of God. Belief in resurrection, however that resurrected life is described, is an essential part of Christianity, and the words of the Anglican funeral service, mirrored in the words of many other Christian Churches, are unequivocal: 'As in Adam all die, even so in Christ shall all be made alive'.

In the Parsee religion also, to which A. and her family belong, death is not the end. As followers of Zoroastrianism, they believe in a Supreme Being, who pervades all life, water, air, fire and earth. After death, the soul is judged and can be sent to 'heaven' or to 'hell'. Some scholars believe that this religion is indeed the precursor of Judaism and Christianity, as many of its beliefs could have been absorbed by the Israelites in their captivity in Babylon where it was the dominant religion. A.'s mother, as a devout Parsee, would have believed, as does her daughter, in a life beyond this one. A.'s use of the prayers for the dead, which she read alone to try to feel some part of the funeral rites taking place in India, show her own adherence to her mother's faith in times of great distress. Her mother's strong faith and her observance of its tenets in everyday life must have given her the assurance her of a life of bliss to follow death.

Such rituals ease the pain of the mourners, helping them to draw a line under the earthly life of the loved one, while also giving them a hope of new life and meaning in that other life. At the same time, the affirmation of the earthly continuity of the social group remaining paves the way for healing, looking to a future in which it will become possible to move on with the living. We have already seen some of the comfort sought in religion by Jane's agonised prayer for her mother to 'be at peace' as she travelled home after receiving the news of her death, and by Poppy's comfort in sharing the last Communion with her mother on the night she died. Although neither Helen nor her mother were deeply religious, the Jewish service of cremation and the rituals which followed were a great comfort to Helen, as were the prayers for the dead which A. used in her far-away home, as her mother's funeral was taking place in India. Jinny, Ana and Judith are all deeply religious, as were their mothers, and this faith was an important element in their experience of death and grief.

For the humanist, the comfort of religious belief that the departed lives on after death with a new status, is a delusion.

Professor John Bowker, writing in his book *The Meanings of Death* describes the humanist vision as one which insists that death is a natural part of life, and which resists what he calls 'the pretensions of religious imagination'. He cites Freud's belief that as human beings developed, they would eventually learn to turn away from the 'fairy tales of religion'.

Nevertheless, the humanist and scientist share with the religious an assertion of the meaning and high value of death. Bowker's humanism is far from a philosophy of despair. He asserts that we can take to those dying or to those bereaved the comfort of knowing that life, as we observe in nature and in science, springs from death; just as surely, death must follow life. The carbon which creates life, for us as for all living things, is derived from the ashes of long-dead stars. Every cell in our bodies is capable of producing an entire new human being, a 'clone' of our biological selves. We are part of a dynamic and beautiful cycle of development through creation and recreation. Life itself, together with the value of all that an individual has been, is never lost. Death has profound value in the ever-developing and growing universe, since without death there could be no new 'architecture of energy'. Thus the humanist can accept quite literally that, in the words of the Anglican service, through death we make of ourselves a 'living sacrifice' for all humanity.

We now look at how the ten women of our witness dealt with the rites of passage for their mother, and how they sought comfort within them. Some of their memories are of funeral and memorial services, others are of private ways of remembering, sorting out their homes, deciding what to do with cooking utensils and other things which symbolise the mother they remember, holding on to treasured and personal possessions, and wearing her clothes.

Anne's story is perhaps the most extraordinary example of a grieving daughter's effort to use her mother's funeral as a source of comfort and healing

> She was going to be cremated, and my father said that we should just have a cheap coffin, but I wanted her to have the best. I knew that she would have wanted that. I wanted to have the funeral in Hartlepool with their friends there, but my father wouldn't go back.

I thought to myself that I would give her the best and most beautiful moments, right to the very end. We had a service in church first, and I bought the best of everything. I filled the church with hundreds of pounds' worth of flowers; some I pretended were from friends, but of course they weren't, because they didn't have many friends in Bristol, all their lives were really in Hartlepool. I chose the order of service carefully. I had 150 programmes printed, even though I knew there would just be four of us there – my father, my two sons and me. I thought 'No way is my mother going to be anything less than superbly beautiful and superbly magnificent. She's going to have everything perfect.' She didn't have a very luxurious life, but this was something I could do for her.

I was trying to bring her back to life in some way in that funeral service, keeping a beautiful woman alive in a beautiful way until the very last minute when her coffin disappeared at the crematorium. I had an organist, a choir and readings – it lasted a long time. I tried to read a poem, but I couldn't get through it and my elder son had to take over. When he got to the part which says 'I have gone into another room' I thought, not yet, Mum, you're still here beside me.

Anne was deliberately refusing to accept that part of the funeral ritual which recognises the new status and locus of the dead. She still finds that hard to do and still finds it hard to move on in her own life.

I wish I could have her back. I feel ashamed that after eighteen months her ashes are still with the funeral director. I don't feel I can come to terms with her death, and I can't cope with what to do. There ought to be a service back in Hartlepool. She was in the Royal Navy during the Second World War and I want to have a ceremony for the disposal of the ashes that would be something grand, and that would include the British Legion flag.

Anne's father died only fourteen months after his wife. He had literally given up the will to live without her. He moved in with his daughter and her younger son, but shut himself in his room with the curtains permanently closed, refused to eat, and sought death as a release. Anne arranged for his funeral near her own home.

I've never been able to clear out their house in Hartlepool. I went back once and everything was exactly the way they had left it. I couldn't bear to touch anything. I just took the hat she had worn long ago at my wedding, took care of all the bills to be paid for utilities and so on and walked away. While I was in the house I kept thinking, 'Why didn't she have more beautiful things?' I will have to face it one day.

Jinny found the rituals after her mother's death much more helpful and healing.

I was able to help my brother to plan the funeral service; we really did it together. I couldn't read at the funeral, I didn't trust myself to get through it. Strangely, though, I didn't cry until after the funeral. It was a release, and I found the ritual helpful. It was good to have all the family there, including my son and daughter who loved her and whom she loved. We had a reception after the service, and I had sorted out her jewellery (my father was a jeweller, so she had some lovely things) and I gave pieces of the jewellery away to the women in the family. It pleased me to be able to do that.

I didn't keep any of her clothes or many of her personal things. Most of them had been dispersed or given away when she moved into the Home for the Blind. I do have all her good silver, and I enjoy looking after it and using it. After the funeral I went straight back to California and carried on with my work. It was a great help to be working and busy.

Judith's mother survived her husband by only one year. Judith and her brother planned the funeral together, and came close in their shared grief.

I couldn't cope without faith, and the service helped me to think about that. She wasn't religious, but she was God-fearing. I am God-loving, and that was something to cling on to in the time after her death. We buried her with my father. After the funeral, I left my brother in their house to say his goodbye. I had already done that during the preparations, and I didn't want to go back. My brother and I wept; we felt like orphans. We cried for ourselves, not for them. We felt comforted that they were together. I felt that at last she was again the free spirit she was meant to be.

I kept just a few of her special things. I kept the saucepan in which she had made her special fish soup. I think she had it all my life. I kept some of her vests and blouses, because I wanted to feel I had something of hers close to me. They began to wear out, and I knew she wouldn't have wanted me to go on wearing them. She never kept things; there was nothing in her drawers and cupboards that wasn't 'here and now, this year's fashion.' She never let us keep things when we were children. So eventually I threw them away. I have a few photographs of her which I love. For her seventy-fifth birthday I paid for her to have one of those special photo sessions where they make you up and use a filter so that you look like a film star. Those are the ones I have kept.

Judith was blessed in that she had a sense of her mother at peace when the funeral was over. Her tears were, as she says, for herself not for her mother.

Simone says of her mother's funeral:

It was spectacular. The entire village turned out. A Scottish village funeral is an amazing experience. I felt completely stunned by it all. In the days before the funeral, the house was always full of people. They came to pay their respects to her as she was laid out in her coffin, but they stayed around all the time. It all seemed quite unreal to me.

I stayed on in the house for a day to clear it out, and it was then I discovered that she hadn't been eating anything for some time. People had given her food, but she had wrapped it up in newspaper and hidden it. For years afterwards I never went near the house; I couldn't bear it. My brother had found her dead, lying on the floor between the bed and the window, and he has never really recovered.

After I had cleared things out, my husband and I drove back

to England in the sunshine in our posh car. I think I went temporarily mad. I told him I was leaving him. I had only stayed married so that she could be proud of me and my handsome rich husband who worked in the City, and our big house and posh car. It really wasn't me. I left my job as well as my husband and went off to Canada. I just went wild.

Simone's choice of what to retain of her mother's possessions tells much of their relationship and of Simone's sense of their shared identity.

I kept my grandmother's wedding ring, which she in turn had wanted my mother to have after her death. I was named after my grandmother, and she was a very special person to me, because of her courage: the Jewish girl abandoned by her family with five children by the age of twenty. I also have my mother's wedding ring. My brother took it at first, as I had the other ring from my granny, but a little while later he came to my house and said I should have it, so now it is mine too and I wear both rings all the time.

The other thing I took is a painting. When my granddad died of the lung disease that so many miners got, the Coal Board paid out compensation to his family. I think my mother's share was about forty pounds, not a lot even then, but to her it was a huge sum. With it she bought not luxuries for herself, but this lovely Japanese painting of green leaves and grass with the light shining through them. Mummy told me, 'I bought it because it is what my father couldn't have. It is light and green things growing in the fresh open air, while he spent all his life in the darkness of the pit. It is a picture of what I would have given my daddy if I could'. I went to University on a scholarship from the National Union of Mineworkers, and it was the Union that fought for my granny to get compensation, so the painting has many meanings of great significance to me.

After the comfort of their final evening together, taking Communion and sitting talking at her bed, Poppy tells of how differently she reacted in the first hours after her mother had died.

Immediately after she died I switched to practicalities. I rang my two brothers to tell them she was gone, and then I rang the undertaker. He didn't arrive until seven a.m., four hours after she died, so I did what I could to make her look good. I even popped her false teeth in.

We arranged the service in church, but I didn't go with her to the crematorium. I didn't want to be there. I stood outside the church and watched the coffin drive away, and I just thought, 'There she is; she has finally gone'. We had a memorial service for her in the North where all the relations could come, and that was a really good occasion.

For Poppy, though, the most important memorial and 'finding' of her mother came a little later when she took her eldest daughter to Stockholm to show her, for the first time, where her grandmother came from.

It was my first visit for forty years, and it was wonderful. I had forgotten how Swedish I was, my Swedish mother's daughter. She had tried to take her identity from my father, but she was so different. All my father's sisters were 'English Roses' while she was so tall and dark and striking.

Perhaps I still haven't really 'let go' of her. Her bedroom is still here, along the hall from my kitchen, full of her things. I've never felt ready to sort them out and throw things away.

A. was away from India when her mother died there, so she was unable to take part in her mother's funeral or in any of the immediate rituals which follow very quickly on death in India. Her marking of ritual waited for a year, when she returned to Bombay for the special ceremony which is held in the Parsee religion on the anniversary of someone's death.

I went for the ceremony, and I hoped it would ease my pain, but it didn't really help. The pain was too personal for that sort of ceremony.

I do have lots of my mother's possessions. I am very sentimental about them, and I can't throw them away. I have her lovely saris and the little tops which she used to have made

105

for her. I wear them sometimes, and sometimes I have them as my pillow, to be close to her. I love wearing her saris. I wore one of them, a particularly beautiful silk sari, so often that in the end it just fell apart because it had got so thin. The same thing happened again when I went to a wedding of a friend wearing my mother's wedding sari. It too had just worn out.

Ana also suffered from not having been present at her mother's funeral and the unexpected nature of her mother's death meant that she, still only in her teens, had no time to prepare for the shock of losing her mother. Having then no opportunity to take part in the rituals of mourning with her family has made it particularly hard to come to terms with her loss.

I was told that hundreds of people turned up for the funeral. As I wasn't there, I missed all that. I felt I had to keep a stiff upper lip even when I did go home to Zanzibar a little later, for the sake of the younger children. I finally broke down and cried when I went to see my aunt. She encouraged me to let my feelings out. I have prayed for my mother's soul every day.

I feel I had never had the opportunity to lay my mother to rest so it took me a very long time to get over it. She was buried in a family plot which my grandfather had bought a long time before.

I didn't have any of my mother's things. Most were sold or lost in the civil unrest in Zanzibar which happened after her death. I was given a photo of my mother, and my husband and I got it framed. It's all I have of her. My sister inherited some jewellery from her, and she has given it to me to keep, but it's not really mine.

For different reasons, Jane too had little opportunity to make arrangements for her mother's funeral.

My sister had made most of the arrangements before I arrived back in England from Italy. She had arranged things for the funeral at my sister's local church and at the crematorium. We knew Mummy wanted her ashes buried in the same grave as our brother John. Mummy had already arranged for her name on his grave, with just the date of her death to be filled in. She had also arranged for our father to be buried in the same grave, but that never happened.

We arranged the burial of the ashes down in Surrey, with the rector of the little church where John was buried. That was a good occasion for me. My two children and my husband were there, and I felt that we were doing something she wanted, so it all felt right.

One of the very bitter things in the time just after her death was what she had written in her will. She had left almost everything to my sister, who is younger than me, and to her children, even things that were of great sentimental value to me. The residue of her estate she left to my husband and not to me and almost nothing to my children. I was very hurt. I have tried to understand it, but it was very hard.

My sister dealt with the sale of Mummy's flat and furniture and she sorted out her clothes and things, so I didn't really have much to do. I have some of her things, not many as she had left them all to my sister and her children, but most precious to me is the book she had written about her life. I am lucky to have that.

Peggy felt so shocked by the way she was treated at the hospital where her mother had died, that she sought some comfort by visiting her mother in the funeral home.

I went to see her. She was like a china doll, lying there. I kissed her, but she was stone cold. We arranged for her to be cremated, like my father. I'm still not sure if that was the right thing. She had not really wanted my father to be cremated, even though he had asked for that, so perhaps she had strong feelings against cremation.

Her funeral was so different from my father's. He had organised everything in advance, and the church was full. Throughout the week before his funeral I had the powerful sense that he was there still, organising things. There was no sense of closure for me with my mother, and her funeral gave me no comfort. My sister did most of the arrangements, and it was not really a good occasion. The vicar even got her name wrong.

He called her 'Elizabeth' which was her first name on the birth certificate, but she had never been called that. I arranged for her ashes to go back to Durham, and we buried them beside my father, as they both would have wanted.

My sister and I went back and emptied out their house. I hired a van and brought back her bedroom furniture and her electric sewing-machine. The machine was a very prized possession of hers, and to me was a symbol of what she had done so well, her gift of dressmaking and tailoring. When I got all her bedroom furniture placed in my bedroom, it looked lovely, and just right for my house. I suddenly found myself wanting to phone her and tell her how good it all looked. I know that's silly, but I thought how pleased she would have been to see it there, in use. I still have all those things, and I still use the sewing-machine.

Helen speaks of the time of her mother's death and burial with deep feeling.

It was a 'one-off' experience. Because it all happened in Australia, and I arrived the day she died, then afterwards I left and came back to my life here, it was like a play, a tableau with a beginning and an end, out of the continuum of the rest of my everyday life. That's why it's so intense and vivid in my memory.

Helen had asked her mother about her wishes for her funeral and burial. Although her mother was not, she feels, deeply religious, nevertheless she embraced her Jewish identity, and felt at home with it. Helen was therefore not surprised when her mother simply said, 'I'm Jewish, so I must be buried Jewish'.

She had made contact with the local rabbi in Melbourne in the last year of her life, and had paid up her dues for membership of the synagogue. I went to see the rabbi, to make the arrangements, and he was wonderful. He wanted to hear all about Mummy, her birth in Poland and life in England, her marriage and family, everything I could tell him. He conducted her funeral in the chapel in the middle of this beautiful park, and for me it was a wonderful occasion. He talked about my mother, using her name often and paying tribute to her many accomplishments. I found the ceremony very comforting. It was a touching and, yes, uplifting experience. I felt as if I was in a trance; I was still jet-lagged, and probably comatose from shock and weariness!

She was cremated, and her ashes are buried in a corner plot in this lovely parkland. It is a perfect place, and I feel that her grave is right for her. She very much wished to be buried beside my stepfather, but he of course was buried in Christian ground, so she knew that would be impossible. If it had been possible, I would have brought her body home to England. As it is, she is buried in the non-orthodox section of the cemetery in Melbourne.

The odd thing is, my birth father had died in Melbourne just a month earlier, and he is buried in the orthodox section of the same lovely parkland. After more than forty years apart, never meeting after their divorce in the 1930s when I was a baby, they are now buried just yards apart in Australia.

Although the rabbi had been such a help in his conduct of the funeral, his later behaviour left much to be desired.

My uncles kept the Jewish tradition of 'Minyan' in which there have to be ten men on duty in the house for seven days of mourning after the death, during the period known as 'Shivah'. The rabbi had agreed to come on one of the nights, to make up the ten, but he didn't turn up, and my uncles were extremely angry. I learned later that the synagogue had also found him wanting, and had refused to renew his contract. Later again I heard that he had converted to Christianity!

After the Shivah I had difficulty getting a flight back to Heathrow, so I stayed on with my aunt and uncle and that was good, because I got to know them better. My uncle was grieving for his little sister as well. I had time to sort out my mother's home and possessions and arranged for a removals company to ship the things I wanted to bring back home. I brought back her desk. It had belonged to my stepfather, and she had shipped it with her to Australia because she loved it.

I use it now. When she bought her house in Melbourne she had bought some lovely new furniture to furnish a room for me. She called it my room as I had promised when she left England that I would come every year to spend time with her. I brought the chest of drawers from it and use that here in my home. I've got lots of her clothes which I wear sometimes and I kept some of her sheets and pillowcases. They all remind me of her.

I have a special drawer for some of her things. In it I have the bras she wore for her prosthesis after her breast was removed when she first had cancer. It may seem odd, but it was a part of the story of the fight she put up at that time of her life, and I keep them to remind me of that. I also have a beautiful dress she made. It was a copy I had asked her to make of a dress she made at the end of the war. It was in eau de nil, and so lovely, and the workmanship is exquisite. It's in the special drawer as well.

She left a will, and in it she had divided up her jewellery amongst the women in the family, her stepdaughter, stepsons' wives and their children. I have her gold chain. She left half of her estate to me and the other half to be divided amongst my two stepbrothers and stepsister.

I arranged for the headstone on her grave. I put my step-father's name and her three stepchildren on it as well as my own. I felt she would have wanted that. I have a photograph of it to remind me of how it looks, as I can't visit there very often. I went back the following year for her Yahrzeit, the anniversary of her death, and attended the service in the syna-gogue when her name was read out. It was again a lovely service, and I felt very good that I had gone.

One ritual element in the weeks after death is the reading of the will. Jane's experience with her mother's will was particularly painful, but for the bereaved the reading of the will can become an important part of the grieving rituals. There is a lawyers' saying that 'Where there's a will there's a war' and all too often it seems as if a family which should be united in grief is instead warring over possessions. Virginia Ironside suggests that this is not necessarily the selfish greed that is often portrayed, but rather because to the bereaved, the possessions of their loved one come to represent the love they have lost.

The daughters have spoken in this chapter about their holding on to small and materially insignificant things which had belonged to their mothers. No one hearing their stories could doubt the importance of the small things which still signify for us the presence and love of our mothers. Small wonder then that daughters invest huge emotion in the wording of the will, the choices made by our mother as to who should inherit various items which had deep significance for those who still need her love. Unwittingly, the writers of wills can cause great pain and sow dissension and envy between siblings, or can convey a last message of love and trust.

Most women report that the rituals following on their mother's death were helpful in the process of grieving, so endorsing the wisdom of our ancestors who devised them. Rites which have been developed over the centuries, and which exhibit so many common elements across different religions and different cultures must have met and still meet the needs of mourners at deep and significant levels. For those who felt excluded or who were absent from the rituals, the grieving process seems to have been more prolonged. As Ana said, 'I had never buried her, so it took me a long time to get over it'. Funerals have an important part to play in the first step towards the long process of grieving.

Wanda Barford, with her unfailingly sure gift for finding words to help and heal, speaks directly to her mother in her poem 'Sky' about the message she felt she had heard from her during the funeral;

> All-round acceptance in that clear and weightless air
> Of things that are and were and pass beyond
> The limits of our bounded life. I heard your voice
> Say: leave me now, I'm perfectly at peace.

Chapter Eight
Grief and Guilt

That I wasn't with you when you died,
Nor heard it when you cried

Falling from your bed;
Nor placed a pillow there beneath your head.

Not to have loosened up your clothes for air,
Nor straightened out your tangled hair.

Not to have said your last *Shema* with you
Who'd taught me it when words were new.

Not to have shut your staring eyes
Nor closed your open mouth; its unheard cries.

And covered your small body;
And covered you as well

With such prayers as I know that mean fare well.
Wanda Barford, 'Regret'

The pain of the early days after the first shock of bereavement is intense. People react in many different ways, but most describe numbness, disbelief and an intensity of feeling unlike any other experience. One woman felt that she regretted leaving this intensity behind, since in it she still felt close to her mother; as the intensity subsided, she felt that her mother was leaving her. Unbearable in some ways though she found the pain, it was better than the dull sense of irretrievable loss which came later when the reality of her mother's death was inescapable.

For me, the weeks after my mother's death were unreal. I felt as if I were locked in a world from which all security and comfort had gone. The loss of my mother seemed impossible to believe or bear. She had always been there, since before I was born, and I had expected her, at some level below reason, to be there always. I wanted to finish the arguments we had as well as to tell her they didn't matter. I wanted her there to share in the good things of my life as well as to comfort me for the bad times. I wanted to say sorry for the times I had not been a good daughter, and I wanted her finally to tell me that she did love me – that she loved me as much as she loved my sister. Now I would never know, and for that and for her loss and for my loneliness, I was inconsolable.

Much has been written by psychologists about bereavement and mourning. One classic study was by Dr Elisabeth Kubler-Ross, who wrote in 1969 of her experiences as a doctor in the University of Chicago in the United States. She criticises the way in which modern western societies have made death less human – 'more gruesome, more lonely, mechanical and dehumanised' as she says, denying the dying patient and the bereaved the simple right to say goodbye and then to grieve as their ancestors were able to do, and making of death a far more frightening thing than its inevitable and human nature should allow. The hospice movement has done wonderful work to try to correct this 'inhuman' way of death, and my sister and I were fortunate in that our mother spent the last two weeks of her life in a hospice which gave both her and us the dignity and care which made death an important part of our lives together.

Kubler-Ross distinguished five stages of grief. These she observed in her dying patients mourning their own death, and then in parallel in those who mourned, both before and after the death of their loved one. Her well known five stages are: denial; anger; bargaining; depression; acceptance. Many others have made later observations which vary the Kubler-Ross formula, and warn that it should not be taken too literally as a necessary progression for all bereaved people, but all broadly accept that grieving does follow stages of emotional and behavioural change, and that these stages may last for days, weeks, months and even in some cases years after bereavement.

The psychologist John Bowlby's much quoted 1961 article on bereavement in the *International Journal of Psychoanalysis* is based on his observations of grieving patients, and offers a description of the stages of mourning which has been widely adopted. He speaks of four stages: numbness, sometimes called denial, in which the reality of death is not appreciated; yearning and searching, in which the urge to find the lost person predominates (and this can last for years); disorganisation and despair, in which the loss finally 'comes home' and is understood; and reorganisation of behaviour, when the bereaved learn to adapt their lives to live on without the presence of the dead.

People respond in different ways to loss, but most psychiatrists and psychotherapists believe that there are common elements in grief, and that the turmoil which follows bereavement is a process. All also agree that the process includes some elements of both anger and guilt.

The early stage of numbness or refusal to accept what has happened is often most strongly accompanied by guilt. For Kubler-Ross, guilt is death's 'most painful companion'. The 'if only . . .' regrets of the bereaved, even blaming some omission or action of their own for the fate of their loved one is all too common, as we have seen already from some of the stories of the ten women interviewed. Many of them, even those with the least evidence of remaining difficulty, still have at least one or two 'if only . . .' regrets which trouble them. E. Lindemann, writing in the *American Journal of Psychiatry* in 1944 said that guilt was a characteristic of what he described as 'normal' grief, along with physical distress and hostility or anger.

Most psychiatrists accept that not only is guilt a part of the first stage of mourning, but so too is anger. The anger which Ana felt towards her father, laying on him the responsibility for her mother's death, was a clear example of this. Jane too felt anger at what she saw as her mother's rejection even after death in the wording of her will. Jane hid much of her anger in personal grief, even blaming herself for her mother's lack of care for her, but the anger was there, and can reappear in uncomfortable ways even now. Anne's anger towards her father for giving up after his wife's death, effectively willing himself to follow her, helped her to deal with some of her own feelings of guilt.

Most psychologists and therapists working with the bereaved accept the model of grief first put forward by Bowlby. An important part of Bowlby's work was the emphasis on the 'searching and yearning' stage, the need of the bereaved to 'find' the person who is lost. While he described the first stage of numbness in sympathetic detail, he believed this was only a short prelude to the much stronger urge towards searching, which can last for many months and sometimes even for years. During this phase, he said, the bereaved thinks often about the dead person, looks for them in places which they associate with them and may privately or publicly use and repeat their name. This strongly resonates with the experience of many women in their searching for their mothers after death. Margaret Drabble, describing her journey 'into the underworld' to find her mother, speaks for many grieving and confused women.

The third stage identified by Bowlby, of disorganisation and despair, when the search is finally abandoned and the bereaved try to accept that the loved one will not be restored, can evoke both anger and depression. Bowlby did not, however, feel that this depression was pathological, as it was a necessary step towards leaving behind the patterns and routines of life which we had with the one we have lost and so getting ready for the next stage, the reorganisation of behaviour, when we learn to rearrange the way we live our lives without the dead person's presence.

Writing in 2001, Dr Dewi Rees, a former Hospice Director and now senior lecturer at Birmingham University, also describes in his book *Death and Bereavement* the first reaction to bereavement as 'numbness and intense pining'. He cites the work of Professor William Worden, a psychologist at the Harvard Medical School, who importantly distinguishes grief from mourning. Grief is an experience, personal and deeply painful; mourning is a process, a process which may be our way of managing grief. Worden believes that in mourning the bereaved faces four 'tasks': to accept the reality of the death of the loved one: to work on the pain and grief such a loss has caused: to adjust to the new reality of a world in which the loved one is no longer present: and to 'emotionally relocate' the deceased person.

In their different language, the psychologists and the anthropologists are telling the same story. Worden's tasks match the purposes of ritual across many societies which we saw in Chapter Seven. The need to 'relocate' the dead person, to confer on them a new identity, and the need to affirm the continuity of the living society for ourselves and our community, which were found to be common to almost all funerary customs, match these identified tasks of adjusting to the world without our loved one, and 'emotionally relocating' the deceased, which are the mechanisms for the management of grief in the bereaved. It seems that our ancestors knew what they needed, as individuals and as a society, and their rituals have been developed in response to human needs over many centuries. It is hard not to feel that those religions and societies which still retain the ancient rituals offer more to the bereaved than do many of the over-regimented and depersonalised routines of bureaucratic hospitals and expensive funeral homes.

While Worden felt that completion of the tasks enabled the bereaved to move on with their lives, not everyone accepts this concept of moving on as a goal for the bereaved. Even the great Sigmund Freud, who in his early work spoke of the need to free oneself from all ties to the lost loved one, in his older years, after his own experience of loss, admitted that such a goal was neither always possible nor always desirable. When he was seventy he wrote to a friend who had lost his son that while the most acute grief will pass 'we also know that we shall remain inconsolable'. A sense of the presence of the dead person can indeed be a normal and life-giving reaction for many, even years after the loss of a loved one. In her often angry book *You'll Get Over It – The Rage of Bereavement* Virginia Ironside criticises the idea of 'getting over it' as unbearably trite. The feeling of bereavement, she believes, will never go away, and 'living with it' is the nearest one can hope for. She is sure that most of the comforting phrases about 'moving on' and 'coming to terms with your loss' are of no real comfort, and may add to the sense of anger and loneliness that the bereaved experience.

Bowlby's third stage, of disorganisation and despair, was, he felt, a necessary if painful way of the bereaved moving towards a new lifestyle without the presence of the person whom they mourn. In the fourth and final stage, the bereaved undertake a reorganisation of their new life without the presence of the loved one. For daughters deprived of their mothers these stages may be more diffuse than for a widow or widower whose life has been intimately bound up with the deceased. Women do not usually lose their mothers until after they have formed a new life with partners, husbands, children and careers. Even Ana, although still a teenager when she lost her mother, had begun her medical training and moved away from home by the time her mother died. Most adult daughters have learned to function perfectly well with relatively little day-to-day contact with their mothers. Forming a new lifestyle is therefore not the priority. The women I interviewed rarely spoke of major adjustments to their routine; all, however, spoke of major changes in their internal landscape of emotion and in doing so they gave shape and form to the unique nature of the mother-daughter relationship.

As the women poured out the stories of their lives with their mothers, as children then as adults, as they spoke of the moment of loss and the weeks, months and years since, a new picture of mourning emerged. The death of a mother brings us as daughters face to face with ourselves as nothing else can do. We find ourselves looking back at memories from long forgotten times, and seeing in them new meanings and understandings of our mothers, and of events long past; we find ourselves confronting the things done and not done in the face of those memories, and what that tells us about ourselves. Sometimes these women spoke of the guilt they feel for the times they looked down on their mother and her lifestyle, even feeling embarrassment about her in relationship to their friends.

Most of all, the women spoke of searching for their mother and for themselves in her. The bond of love, tenderness, guilt, anger and identity which daughters and mothers share from the moment of the birth of a woman to a woman, is never stronger than when the mother dies. Alone for the first time without her mother as a backdrop to her life, almost every daughter experiences a need to find who and what she is, and how much of her

117

mother survives in her, even in ways she may have wished to ignore or repudiate during her mother's life. For a daughter, as we have seen, the mother, and therefore also her death, seem to have a profoundly deep significance beyond the common experience of grief. Searching for our mothers is a search for ourselves.

A very different experience of loss occurs for daughters whose mothers, for whatever reason, have given them inadequate mothering in life. One of the most extreme stories of such a mother is told in the autobiography of Paula Fox. In *Borrowed Finery* she tells of how she was virtually abandoned by her parents from birth. Although there is much in the book which appals in the account of her mother's mental cruelty, yet one feels at times that the writing of the book is itself a search for the mother and for some healing understanding of her mother's behaviour.

Throughout her childhood Paula was passed around amongst relatives and friends of her parents, sent from State to State and country to country at the whim of her father who had divorced her mother and married again. Catching only brief glimpses of either parent, for at most a day or two at a time every few years, she was forced to create an emotional life for herself which excluded her parents. Her weak and handsome father, a Hollywood script writer who knew all the famous names of the era, showed her occasional casual kindness, but she suffered repeated and cruel rejections from her mother Elsie, who made no secret of her dislike of her daughter's presence. As an adult, Paula broke all contact with her mother, seeing nothing of her for thirty-eight years.

When Paula's mother was ninety-two and dying, Paula's children urged her to go and visit her mother before she died. They gave their grandmother Paula's phone number, and Elsie then called, and spoke to Paula in her 'seductive, familiar voice'. Paula agreed to go to visit her in Nantucket, where she now lived. Even then, her mother could not show any affection or interest in Paula's life, and in a characteristic act of cruelty, showed Paula a photograph of her father, Paula's grandfather, which she said she wanted Paula to have. She then hid it while her daughter was out of the room, so Paula could only have it if she begged her mother to give it to her. Although Paula wanted the photograph – a tenuous link with the identity of her mother – she refused to beg, and so the photograph was lost to her.

Paula describes her 'revulsion' at her mother during this last visit as being so intense that she could not even bring herself to use the same toilet that her mother might have used, so she went into the field outside the house to urinate. She escaped to catch an earlier train, glad to be gone. When she was told of her mother's death a few months later, she says she could only feel 'hollow, listless'. She comments that she, who had been denied so much of a daughter's experience, had now lost what she describes as a daughter's last privilege, the right to mourn a mother.

Nancy Friday feels that forgiving our mothers for their inadequacies is the hardest, but most important task we face before or after their death. She quotes Dr Richard Robertiello, who believed that it is important to recognise the 'bad mother' parts of our childhood experiences of mothering. Unless we recognise them, and forgive them, we shall forever feel that we ourselves were to blame for the deficiencies in mothering and in the love which we so craved. Admitting and facing our mother's human failings, and loving and holding to those parts of her which were good and adequate for our needs, enables us as daughters to get on with our own lives, accept those parts of us which we got from the 'good' as well as the 'bad' mother, and try to do better in our turn.

Several examples of the guilt our women felt were to do with the arrangements they had made in putting their mother into a home for the elderly when they became unable to look after themselves. Jinny, Helen and Jane all express some discomfort with the decision they had to make towards the end of their mother's lives. All emphasise, rightly, that their mothers had encouraged and fostered their careers, and giving up their work to care for a sick mother would have meant an end to their mother's ambitions for them as well as their own. In Jane's case, her mother would have been the first to emphasise that her first duty lay with her husband whose job took them away to Germany and then Italy in the last years of her mother's life.

This dilemma is one likely to become routine for the next

119

generation, since almost all our daughters are undertaking heavy commitments in their careers, in contrast to our mothers' generation, who often did accept that they would be their own mother's last carer. I feel very confident that there are very few mothers of my feminist generation who would for one moment contemplate the thought of our daughters interrupting the career of which we are so proud in order to take care of us in old age.

Of course, provisions for care of the elderly are now so much better and more preserving of dignity than were the alternatives to home care in our grandmothers' day. Sheltered housing, which leaves the elderly with privacy and self-determination, is a profitable and growing market. Hospices, which offer to the dying the benison of pain management and death with dignity and peace, have offered a blessed alternative to the nightmare visions of hospital deaths in impersonal wards with doses of mind-destroying morphine the only relief.

Like so much of our misplaced guilt, the doubts experienced by daughters whose mothers died in homes reflect more of their own grieving process than of the reality of their mother's feeling or wishes.

Genie Zeiger, in her book *How I Find Her*, explores this dilemma from her own experience in painful detail. Genie discovered that her mother had become incontinent and confused when she came to visit Genie and her husband not long after the death of Genie's father. When Genie's husband suggested that they should have her mother to live with them, Genie replies 'I'd die', hating herself for saying it as she does so.

Genie describes with frank self-understanding how she argues with herself in the next few months, trying to justify her decision by reminding herself that her mother put *her* mother into a nursing home in her last years. She knows well the difference for her mother between being 'in' a home and being 'at' home. She admits, though, that although she wants to be the kind of woman who gives up her life to care for her mother, she knows in her heart that she would fail if she tried.

Genie's guilty feelings stay with her for a long time, but in the last weeks and days of her mother's life, when she was with her in her dying almost constantly, the guilt was healed. She had taken hospice training in order to help her mother and herself through the last stages, and took an active role, emotionally and physically, in the care of her mother.

Zeiger's decision to write the book of her mother's dying and death was at first in order to survive her grief and then later to show other women both that a daughter's deep and overwhelming grief at the death of her mother is 'normal', and also that it is possible to find 'redemption' at the end. For her, the redemption came in the care she was able to show to her mother in sharing her last days, and in the unbelievably difficult time of sharing her mother's decision to refuse food at the end, so as to end her suffering. Redemption, for Genie, meant finally a new relationship with the divine; not, she says, the Jewish God of her childhood, as she has discovered a more feminine and less angry God than that. Still she recites now the Jewish prayers of her childhood, and in this new faith she finds that promise of redemption. This was her mother's last gift to her in dying.

Much comfort or pain can be derived from the immediate arrangements for formal leave-taking with the dead, and from the conduct of funerals and memorials. As we have seen, Genie Zeiger's story of the rites of preparing her mother's body for burial, which she and other women shared, is a most moving example of this. Virginia Ironside also speaks from personal experience when she talks of the function of a Christian funeral as being, amongst other things, to tell the bereaved that the person *is* dead, and to 'ram home' the message that everyone attending the funeral will know this as well. Any arrangements for the immediate rituals can have resonance in the later stages of mourning, making the path either more difficult or easier for the bereaved.

Ironside emphasises the importance of seeing the person after death. This view also derives from her own and others' personal experience. She feels that seeing the body of your loved one helps in accepting the reality of their death. For some, she says, the sight of the 'empty shell' offers a kind of peace, that the loved person has gone from the body, and is therefore still living, but not in the bodily sense. Ironside tells of one woman's experience of seeing her mother at the funeral chapel, and finding with some surprise that there was nothing there – just an empty body. She felt most powerfully that her mother could not be there in that dead flesh and bone, but must be 'somewhere else'. Although not a believer in a sure afterlife, she felt a sudden certainty that there must be another place where her mother's spirit still survived. For others, there is the joy of seeing the pain of the last weeks or months of suffering gone from the face of their loved one, and turned into a relaxed and peaceful countenance.

Simone talked endlessly to her dead mother – telling her all the things she had planned to say to her in life. Peggy kissed the 'china doll' which her mother's cold face had become. Poppy sat alone with her mother for some hours, making her look good, popping her false teeth in place while she waited for the undertaker. Helen rejoiced at seeing her mother look again at peace and surprisingly young, while Anne felt that she had to come physically close to her mother's body again in the period after she died because of 'the procedures you have to go through'. Jinny too felt that her mother's peaceful face in death was a last message of comfort. Judith had seen her mother just before she died, and that for her was enough.

The three women who did not see their mother after death sometimes regret that, and wish now that they had. Jane feels regret that, by the time she arrived home from Italy 'the undertaker had taken over and I didn't even see her'. Ana and A. both feel real pain that they were neither able to take part in their mothers' funerals, nor to say goodbye to them properly. A. feels sadness still that the rites for her mother's death were 'all going on in Bombay and I was here in England'. Ana says 'I never laid her to rest, and so it took me a long time to get over it'. Their experience underlines the value of the formal opportunities to recognise and accept the reality of death in helping with the earliest period of grief.

Whatever the experience at the time of death, grief mixed with anger and guilt seem to have had a part in the feelings of the bereaved women for some days or weeks afterwards. Anne tormented herself with a conviction that she was somehow responsible for her mother's death because she had taken the pearls which her mother insisted she should have. The occasion is very revealing, as we have seen, since for Anne's mother, the gift of the pearls – originally Anne's gift to her mother – may have symbolised her wish to pass on to her daughter this most precious possession while she was still alive. Anne's love of and need for her mother made her unwilling to face the thought of losing her, and therefore reluctant to accept the pearls her mother offered. Later, after her mother's death, in grief and confusion, she says, 'If only I hadn't taken the pearls, perhaps she'd still be here'.

Anne's efforts to give her mother the best of everything in death, while largely motivated by love and grief, had within it an element of what Virginia Ironside has called making up for the things you feel you didn't do for the dead person in life. Anne's 'if only . . .' expressed a host of regrets which she, like so many grieving daughters, suffer when their beloved mother is no longer there to share, argue, annoy and forgive. The apparent sudden nature of her death left Anne doubly grieving, both for her loss and for the absence of any period to say proper goodbyes. The chance to 'say what needs to be said' before the final parting is very precious, and can assuage some of the sharper pain of the first period of grief.

Anne describes her feelings during the funeral service. 'I was trying to keep her here with that service. I still don't feel I have come to terms with it. I so wish I could have kept her here.' Eighteen months after her mother's death, Anne was still in the first stage of grief; she was full of guilt, and anger at what had happened, as well as turning some of her anger against her father who had failed to give her any sense of support and shared grief. He had shut himself away from life, lived in darkness and waited and willed for death. Anne's sense that her family had fallen apart after the death of their much-loved wife, mother and grandmother is an extreme example of the disruptive power of grief when the guilt and anger are unresolved.

Judith was spared much of both guilt and anger after her mother's death, in part because she had time to prepare herself for her loss in the year before her mother died. It was helpful that she and her mother had been able to talk together and acknowledge the fact of her dying. Judith also feels that her strong Christian faith has helped her.

> I couldn't cope without faith. I feel now she has got rid of her body and become the free spirit she always was. My grief was

for myself, not for her. I wept copiously because I was an orphan – I really did feel like an orphan child. There were no regrets or 'if only' thoughts. We had said everything that needed to be said. It was important to me that I had talked to her about how I would cope after she died. She had given me the reassurance I needed when she said, 'I'll be there. I'll be the first star you see at night.' That was a wonderful gift of comfort to me in the period after she died.

Simone admits that she 'went wild' in the period after her mother's death. It was almost brutally sudden, and Simone had had little time to prepare herself, or have the kind of conversation with her mother which she so desperately needed and wanted. The shock of hearing the news from policemen, and facing the crowded house of mourning villagers back in Scotland, made the whole period a nightmare. Simone speaks of the rage and wildness she felt for some considerable time, and knows that she was in total denial. Both rage and guilt whirled around with the grief in her. In Canada, she says, she flung herself into many different loveless affairs, in an attempt to bury her grief.

For Simone, her mother's death was literally the end of one life and the beginning of another. Her decision to leave her husband, her job and her country immediately after the funeral was her way of dealing with overwhelming grief. She feels that much of her life up to that point had been lived for her mother, to make her proud of Simone's accomplishments.

At a much deeper level, Simone had been doing the things her mother had been denied, such as attending the good grammar school, going away to university, living down in England. Simone was deeply affected by the vision of her mother 'looking out of the window towards England and what it represented: escape from her restricted life'. Because of her deep love for her mother, Simone absorbed those longings, and felt the need, through her own accomplishments, to give back to her mother the achievements she had been denied. She married her rich husband and lived in her 'posh' house so that her mother could vicariously enjoy this lifestyle, and have something to boast about to her friends in the village.

Simone was living the life she felt her mother should have had, not her own life. At the same time, Simone was aware, painfully aware after her mother's death, that her achievements and lifestyle had separated her from her mother. She had to leave her friends to be with her mother; the two could not comfortably mix. It was to be a long time before Simone could complete the long journey of finding and accepting all the versions of the mother she had lost. In the process she found a stronger version of herself.

Poppy still has some feelings of anger, although stronger in the re-telling than on any frequent occurrence in the present. She has a real sorrow that the call from her mother's nurse to tell her that the end was near could not be put through to her because the telephone extension had been left off the hook. The nurse had to run to get her, but she reached her mother's bedside minutes too late to be with her as she died. In moments of recall, the anger and regret of that last failure are still palpable. There is also still a moment of remembered anger when Poppy recalls her mother's attitude towards her daughters. 'Mother wasn't really nice about my daughters. She even compared them unfavourably with me. I think that's very indicative.' No other negative feelings survive from the painful period of her mother's death. As Judith had also found, the long time she and her mother had together to prepare for their parting was immensely helpful.

This grieving in advance, which psychologists call anticipatory grief, can be enormously beneficial, and can help both the dying and the bereaved, in that it both allows important things to be said and fears to be expressed and shared. It also prepares the bereaved for some of the feelings which will overwhelm them when the moment of loss finally arrives.

Helen had prepared herself with 'anticipatory grief' to some extent, but not enough to cushion her from the numbness of shock which followed on her mother's death. Her poignant account of the last real parting from her mother, outside the nursing home in Australia, is unquestionably an account of mother and daughter both feeling that this was a last goodbye, and searching for the words to say. The months that followed, however, were not easy. Helen's mother became confused and wrote letters begging to come home, which caused then, and still cause today, intense feelings of guilt in Helen.

Helen's feelings of guilt emerge in her silent response to her mother saying, on that last occasion, 'You have been a very good daughter'. 'No,' Helen says now, 'I wasn't a good daughter to her. If I'd asked her to come to live with me instead of going off to Australia, I think she would have done. When she was having her first round of chemotherapy in Melbourne, she asked me, ''Would you give everything up to come and look after me?'' I find that hard to think about now.'

Helen's guilt is reinforced by the assumption of her aunts and uncles in Australia that 'something had gone wrong', that there must have been a quarrel between her and her mother, to induce them to settle for living so far apart in the latter years of her mother's life. The guilt too involves her choices in life, and her conviction that these distressed her mother. The career she chose as a doctor, when her mother wanted her to be an accountant; her marriage to an older, non-Jewish husband and their wedding in a church; above all, the failure to have children, and, in that, denying what she describes as her mother's immortality; all these now cause her guilty pain.

Helen covers her pain by fighting back in an unspoken argument with her mother about her shortcomings. 'Mummy did not put me first; she put her marriage to my stepfather first. She didn't bring me up herself; she left me in Wales and went off for a year or more.' These true feelings help her to put the relationship in perspective, but the guilty feelings still distort some of the memories, and the deep love there was between her and her mother cries out for recognition again and again as she speaks of their times together. Helen, with many, many other bereaved daughters who still experience guilt in their feeling towards their mother, says with the author Margaret Drabble 'night and day on me she cries'.

Like Judith, A. also cried for herself as an orphan when she was told the news that her mother had died. 'I didn't cry so much for her. I felt that she was free again after all she had suffered.' A. still feels some guilt about her life-choices. 'I still feel that I had cheated Mummy by coming to England and having her grandchild here. I think she had to fight her sadness that I left her to

live in England.' A. and her brother, both of course in the first
'angry' stage of grief, had a painful and angry argument in the
weeks after their loss. 'My brother accused me of not taking my
share of our mother's care. He was angry, and a lot of old resentments came out. That was really painful. Now we are very close
again, and that would have pleased her.'

There are strong echoes in what some women said with the
academic quoted in the opening chapter, who said with much
pain that she wished she could now seek her mother's forgiveness
for the unrecognised cruelty she and her siblings had inflicted on
her because during her lifetime she had been 'a joke' to her
daughters. In the same vein, some of the ten women long for an
opportunity to say things to their mothers which they have only
learned after their death.

Peggy is still mourning in many ways. Her guilt is that of
many successful women of her generation who dismissed their
'housewife' mothers as of little importance.

I didn't feel any closure with Mummy after her death. When
Daddy died, I felt he was still there, organising things as he
always had, for the funeral. When his casket moved off through
the curtains I felt he'd gone; there was closure; he and we
were satisfied. It was so different with Mummy. There was no
sense of it all being right.

Now she's gone, I just so wish I had talked to her – properly
I mean, to find out more about her feelings and give me a
chance to understand her, hear her story. I learned so much
about her after she died. She was so strong and taught me so
much; I wish I'd said that to her. I would love to tell her now
how much I have come to understand her. I don't think I ever
bothered while she was still alive.

Jane's feelings contain a combination of still-raw grief, anger
and guilt. Her mother's behaviour in the last years of her life
caused a great deal of pain and anger for Jane. The terms of
her mother's will are still beyond comprehension, and Jane is
tormented with the search for reasons why her mother should
effectively have cut her, and her children, out of the will, leaving
almost everything to Jane's younger sister, and leaving the residue

127

of her estate to Jane's husband. This was hard to accept from the mother to whom throughout life she had been so close, and to whom she believed she had in every conceivable way been a good and supportive daughter. Jane and her mother had lived together, with Jane as the bread-winner, for the years after Jane's graduation until her marriage. Jane had earlier supported and helped her mother in running her hotel business, often undertaking menial and physically demanding tasks, throughout her undergraduate years.

At the same time, Jane feels guilty that she saw so little of her mother in the last years of her life. Because she lived abroad, that is understandable, but Jane regrets that even on her last visit home, she only visited her mother twice, finding the visits too upsetting to want to repeat the experience. Jane's exclusion – because of circumstance – from the arrangements for the funeral and her failure to see her mother after death have also left her with a feeling that there was no proper goodbye. Of all ten women, Jane has perhaps the hardest burden to bear, and although it is evident that she has still many confused and difficult emotions to cope with, the fact that she has accomplished so much since her mother's death is a testament both to her own strength, and to the enduring strength of her earlier relationship with her mother.

Ana's feeling, as we heard earlier, was that because of the suddenness of her mother's death, 'I felt I'd never buried my mother'. Far away from Africa, she was excluded from all the rituals and formal farewells, and had to deal with her grief alone in Ireland. Her anger at her father lasted for thirty years, and she still has real though unnecessary feelings of guilt because, like many teenagers away from home, she didn't bother to write often to her mother while she was away in Ireland, not even to thank her for the gifts and cakes she sent. She says sadly, 'I wondered if I'd done right by her. I did feel guilty when she died. I was just so busy with my own life.'

The process of mourning took longer because of the way she had to come to terms without the healing rituals, but discernibly she moved over the years from shock and numbness, through a searching to understand, as an adult woman herself, the woman her mother had been. The final stage of grieving was achieved by her accepting that she would have to move through all the stages of adult life, her graduation and qualifying as a doctor, her marriage and the birth of her children, without the support of her mother and without the sharing of pleasure with her in all these major life events which she would so have loved to have had. Like Jane, and for such different reasons, she has had to find her own strength in life, but in finding that strength she has also been able to draw on the strength of the good and happy relationship she had with her mother in the early years of her life, and in their shared faith.

Although Jinny reassures herself that her mother would never have wanted her to give up her career, she does 'deeply regret' the decision to put her mother into a home in the last years of her life. Like so many of the other daughters, she also regrets that she was not present when her mother died. She says with emphasis, 'I *so* wish I'd stayed with her that day'. Such regrets plague so many of the women who talked to me, and yet the reassurance of hospice workers that the dying often seem to wait to die until their nearest loved ones have left the room is surely of comfort. It is significant that Jinny's mother, like the mothers of Helen, Poppy and Judith, waited for their daughters to come to them, hold their hand and speak in the voices they wanted to hear one last time. Once that goodbye had been said – even silently – they were able to let go and die in peace.

Hospice workers suggest that this phenomenon is because to die in the loved one's presence is, for some people, just too difficult. The pain of leaving loved ones, with which the dying must come to terms, and the sadness of relinquishing a final contact is for some easier when the physical presence has been removed, even if only over a short time and distance. In the end, no matter how close and how loving our family and friends may be we each of us must die alone.

Simone puts this starkly when she says of the way that her mother died alone in Scotland, without waiting for her daughter to come, 'I realise now it was the most loving thing she could have done. There was no way we could ever have said goodbye.'

Once again, Wanda Barford speaks for us all as daughters in the early tasks of mourning, when we must use such strengths

as we have, often those strengths our mothers gave us, to overcome the darkness of loss:

> When I awoke she'd left
> And darkness invaded the room
> Like the ending of a chapter . . .
>
> I fought it with all the resources
> She had so diligently
> Taught me to muster.
>> from Wanda Barford, 'After a Visit'

Chapter Nine
Loving in Finding

You're passing into me.
I hear my mouth pronouncing your words
I hear my breath breathing you.
　　　from Wanda Barford, 'Becoming You'

The eleventh-century theologian and Archbishop of Canterbury, St Anselm, speaking of his search for God said, 'I find Thee in loving and love Thee in finding'. The passionate 'yearning and searching' which psychologists describe as present in mourning can offer the same joyous outcome for daughters who seek to find their mothers after death. Certainly, it takes acknowledged need and perhaps in some cases a love still unacknowledged to undertake the search for our mother; the reward of the search, as I myself have found, is to discover the love, both ours and hers, even where it may have been well and deliberately hidden before.

It was years after my mother's death that I found myself remembering incidents which brought vividly home to me the loving things she had done, and the planning and thought that had gone into them. I remembered how she had moved out of her comfortable bed when I went to stay with her, so I could have 'the best'; how she had shopped to buy the foods which were my favourites for the meal when I arrived. I remembered how lovingly she had hurried to make jam from the blackberries she and I and my children had picked together on one occasion, and the pride with which she showed me the jars of perfectly made preserve, ready in time for our leaving. As those memories came flooding back, I found myself saying out loud, 'Mummy *did* love me'.

Even now, years after her death, I still see flashes of her in my own behaviour towards my children, and think, 'That's why she did or said that – I understand now'. More important, I am beginning now to understand how she felt – how as age and the thoughts of mortality crept up on her, she needed my love every bit as much as I needed hers.

The women I interviewed have also all found themselves getting to know and understand their mothers in new and better ways after their death. Some did this consciously and deliberately, searching for a mother they realised they did not know as well as they now wished to do; others found incidents and memories suddenly illuminating aspects of their mother's personality or their relationship to her. Recognising strengths in their mother they had not seen before, perhaps because of the context in which those strengths were exercised, and able also to acknowledge their mother's sexuality, which had before been a forbidden subject for many, they were able to identify with aspects of their mother not understood before.

Some bereaved daughters have had to confront the negative traits in their mother's personality, and in her behaviour as a mother and wife, but in confronting these, some have found an opportunity for forgiveness. Facing up to the justifiable anger we felt and may still feel, but recognising that our mothers were human, with human problems, needs and weaknesses for which we were not responsible, can liberate us and deliver us from the feelings of guilt towards her, and from the unattractive tendency to blame our own shortcomings and failures on our mother rather than on ourselves.

I was struck by the number of times I heard each say, 'I am my mother: I recognise that. I am becoming more like her every day.' In their earlier days, when their mothers were still alive and her minor irritating habits were predominant in their minds, such a statement would probably have been unlikely. In the peaceful recognition and maturity which they have reached after their mother's death, recognising how much of her is in them was no longer a matter for concern; rather, it bestowed a sense of continuity, a sense that she was not lost. Psychologists warn us that in some unsatisfactory relationships 'becoming our mothers' can be a daughter's way of compensating for still-unresolved feelings of guilt; we may be trying to keep her alive in ourselves as a way of compensating for some perceived fault of our childhood. Yet in most cases the opposite is true. In acknowledging our debt to our mother, and accepting how much of her is in us, we become liberated and accepting of ourselves.

In the closing chapter of Margaret Foster's book *The Memory Box*, where she tells the story of Catherine's search for the mother she lost as a baby, following the clues of the memory box which was her mother's legacy to her, we see Catherine reflecting on the end of her search. By undertaking the search for her mother which the box inspired Catherine gladly recognises that she is now 'complete' because at last she is 'connected' to her mother. At times, thinking about the contents of the box, Catherine finds herself flooded with emotion. She realises that during the year she spent searching for her mother she had concentrated on her to the exclusion of everything else, with 'constant thoughts' of her mother. If this sounds all like the yearning and searching which daughters undertake immediately after the loss of their mother, so we may conclude that Catherine was experiencing the familiar stages of grief, but over thirty years after her mother's death.

Catherine found sufficient love to undertake her own journey of finding, and then, in finding, love for the mother she found. Now, she says, she can move on with her life, feeling complete as never before. Emerging from the numbness she had felt after the death of her father and stepmother, she finds that she can feel again, that her mother's past has been 'put in front of me and dealt with'. The love she finds at the end of her search leads her also to wish to perform some of the rituals which other bereaved daughters have found helpful. She visits the crematorium on the anniversary of her mother's death, and debates about whether to give her mother a memorial. Eventually she decides, admitting the sentimentality of her decision, to have a small, hand-crafted silver box made in memory of her mother, lined in velvet and just large enough to contain the necklace she had found in the box, but small enough for her to carry it with her wherever she went. The reason for this choice is, as she says, 'for the comfort of it'. Like the memory box her mother left for her baby daughter, it soothes pain and communicates beyond the separation of death.

The daughter of one of the victims of the terrible Dr Shipman, who was convicted of murdering so many of his elderly patients, was interviewed recently on BBC radio. She is clearly a brave woman, offering an example of determination not to allow either her mother's memory or her family's life to be destroyed by this terrible experience. She told the interviewer with courageous assurance, 'Mother will still be part of the family'. She went on to explain her conviction that her mother would be alive in the memories of her children and grandchildren who loved her. Conviction that the lost one lives on in this new but still-loved and vital form is an important element in moving on from loneliness, yearning and grief.

Many people report an experience of the actual presence of the person they love, sometimes several months after their death. This is not in the sense of any psychic phenomenon, seeing a ghost or spirit, just a strong sense that the person they love is still near them. Such experiences of a 'sense of presence' are no longer regarded as signs of mental imbalance, but are recognised as a normal feature of bereavement. Professor Dewi Rees describes his own research on the subject as revealing that these 'sense of presence' experiences, largely unsought by the bereaved, seldom included any physical touch or sound, but are powerful and convincing to the bereaved, who generally find them to be both pleasant and helpful.

Gene Zeigler speaks of her mother's presence as hovering in her home like a helium balloon hanging on the ceiling for several weeks after her death. The presence left her, suddenly and completely one day and the house felt free and open again. Kate Millett in words most lovely pays tribute to her mother's continuing presence in her and in all her family, saying 'She enters and dwells within'. To the mother who is no longer physically present, she does not need to say any farewell, only 'Welcome!'

For many, perhaps all daughters, such a sense of presence can be very real. The mother who has been a part of their lives since before their birth remains present in so many ways in small things as well as large. I think of Simone, wrapping 'the cloak of her mother' round her when going into intimidating and important meetings; Helen saying 'In some ways I am my mother. I can see her looking out through my eyes even as we speak about her', and Peggy, 'Now I catch myself in the mirror and it's her!' Poppy keeps her mother's room just down the hall from her kitchen, for the comfort of her remembered presence.

In some of the stories our women tell, it is apparent that the assigning of a new place and role to their dead mother is to recognise how much of them is still there in them, even in her ways of doing things around the home, and in her methods of child rearing. Several women, recalling something their mother had done with them, commented, 'I do that with my children now'. In this way, they recognise that their mother is still a part of the family life, but as one remembered and present in them rather than as a living or even a 'missing' person in any sad way.

Coping with the last two of the 'tasks' of grieving which were described by Professor William Worden is never straightforward. In Chapter Eight we saw something of how the bereaved women managed the first two tasks, the acceptance of the reality and working through the pain. Now we look at how the bereaved can adjust to a world without the loved one, and 'relocate' them, grant them a new and different status in their lives, so as to move on.

The place of burial can be a focus for personal ritual of remembrance and tribute to the loved one, as well as a help in relocating them in a new and different status. Today many cremations take place without any burial or identifiable place where the deceased lie, but for others, whether the disposal has been a burial of the ashes or a conventional burial of the body, the grave can assume a meaningful function in the continuing life of the bereaved. A recent research study by Francis, Kellaher and Neophytou of 1,500 people who were interviewed as they visited graves in six outer London cemeteries revealed the strong significance which visiting and tending such places held for the bereaved and for the community from which they come.

The researchers found that special days attract the bereaved as appropriate times to visit. For many, the major 'family' occasions such as Christmas, Mother's Day and Father's Day, birthdays, or for Muslims the end of Ramadan are considered special days to visit the grave. They also found that the visiting of graves is seen as a part of sustaining family relationships. The dead are assigned their place in family occasions and this loving duty and need stretches across generations, providing a focus for the continuity of the family.

For the majority of those visiting, the time at the grave is an opportunity to think about and sometimes talk to the deceased. Some share news of the family, or ask for guidance in decisions they have to make. The researchers quote women saying things such as, 'I talk to my Mum and tell her the news,' or 'I come to remember my mother . . . to honour her,' 'I cherish her more since she died'. One visitor expressed the significance of the visit by describing the cemetery as the place where she could 'get her emotions together'.

Just as rituals are an important part of the mourning process in the days after death, so ritual can be an important way of dealing with the process of remembering and assigning a new place to the dead in the years which follow. Many religions offer a special celebration of the deceased on at least the first anniversary of their death, and often later anniversaries too. Both A. and Helen travelled long distances to attend such services for the anniversary of their mother's death. Most of the women spoke of how they remember their mother with a special intensity on the anniversary of her death, and some also spoke of the times of year, like Christmas, when the memories of past times with their mother are particularly meaningful. Christian churches have prayers for the dead in their regular intercessions and many remember by name those whose anniversary has fallen in that week.

Our ten women have each in different ways and with different degrees of success learned to carry on living successful lives without a living place for their mother. Most have succeeded in finding a new and different place for her in their lives, a new status for her, often by a recognition of how much of her is present in them, in their ways of mothering or performing daily tasks, even in the values and faith which she taught them. For some, most powerfully, their mother's dying has permitted recognition of their love for her and a new peace with themselves and the women they are.

A. speaks of her mother as 'free again'. After long struggles with diabetes and the debilitating conditions it brought, A. feels that in death her well and happy mother was restored and free. She also discovered something wonderful about her mother's love for her. 'I used to worry that she didn't love me, but after she died people told me that she talked about me all the time, and loved me a lot. That helped me very much. Now, I think she did love me.'

A.'s feelings for her mother appeared movingly in a dream the night before I interviewed her. She told me, 'Last night I was thinking about her before I talked to you and I had a dream. I was sitting in a sort of space ship, up in the air, and my mother was driving it. We were both very free, and she was laughing, and loving the chance to drive it. She loved driving, and always drove very fast. It was such a happy dream.'

A. reflects on how she managed to complete the tasks of mourning, and come to terms with the loss of her mother, even though suffering greatly from the sadness of being unable to attend her funeral. 'It was just time that helped me to get on. There is a firm belief in life after death in the Parsee religion. We can go to pray in the Fire Temple. I believe there is a future, something after death.'

Peggy has spent some time after her mother's death in the search for her.

I have learned so much about her since she died. Looking through her things afterwards I found so much that I hadn't known or hadn't bothered about, like her 'reciting'. I learned of her pride in her own mother that was apparent from the way she had written 'manageress' on the photograph. I wish now I could tell her how much I understand. I am like her, I can see that now. People used to confuse our voices on the phone, and now I catch myself in the mirror sometimes and it's her! I get my 'stroppiness' from her – in the best sense. I feel I *can* do things. She did things a man was supposed to do, like running a big household without my Dad, and she taught me that. Thanks to her, I really knew that a woman could do anything she set her mind to.

Finding out about her after her death has helped me in so many ways. I understand her and all she did for me so clearly, and I have come to recognise her in me. I still wish I could talk to her and tell her, and I wish I'd talked to her more when she was alive.

Despite some lingering self-doubt about her mother moving into a home in the last years of her life, Jinny has not a single 'bad' memory of her mother to disturb her now. Knowing that she had fulfilled all her mother's hopes for her, and with the assurance that they had enjoyed a lifetime of love and trust, Jinny has much to be thankful for. She says

> I was prepared for my mother's death, but after she died I kept seeing her in myself. She was there when I looked in the mirror, and in the things I was doing. I'd think I was doing them the way she had done them, and so she was there.
> After her death, it was a great help to be working and busy. That helped me to get on with life. I still dream about her a lot. In my dreams she is always younger, and we have fun together. Her death made me look at my relationship with my daughter. So much of the first relationship of my mother and me has gone into that relationship. She was my model, and she was the rock.

Judith has a clear vision of how much she has learned by the experience of her mother's death. As one of the women who always saw herself as 'Daddy's girl' she was never too close to her mother as a child. Like many other such women she now says of her mother, 'Now she's dead, I feel I'm getting to know her. I was embarrassed by so many things about her when I was young, but now I've come to respect her. I feel that now she's dead, she has got rid of her body and become the adventurous free spirit she always was in her youth.'

Judith has also found understanding of herself in gaining respect for her mother. 'Now I have an affectionate recognition of who my mother was. I finally understand what sort of woman she was and therefore what sort of woman I am. I'm very comfortable with that. Because she and I had been through such a lot together, in her later years there was a mutual female respect between us.'

The many roles women play in their families can also be

handed down from mother to daughter. Judith feels this in her role with her adult son. 'Now my son is married, I think about her as she was as a mother-in-law to my brother's wife. I think I'd like to be like her in that role.

'I have no regrets; no longer anything I wish were different. We had said everything to each other that needed saying.'

Even now, Simone feels many sadnesses about her mother. She still regrets that she didn't tell her mother about her marriage until after it had happened, and that after her marriage to a rich Englishman, her mother was never comfortable with Simone's 'posh' friends. She feels shame that her mother spent her time in their house cleaning and cooking. Simone knew that her mother would not leave Scotland to come to live with her and her husband. 'I think she was probably right. It wouldn't have been right for her, and I didn't really want her running my life. I had to leave my friends to be with her. I think my daughter feels that way now about me and her friends.' She also regrets that she never talked to her mother about her mother's lover. Although Simone's father had died when her mother was a young woman of thirty-nine, Simone was not comfortable with her need for another relationship. She speaks now of 'the sexuality I could not face'.

As a mother herself, Simone recognises how much of her identity stems from her mother. 'I felt I met my mother again when I became a mother. I feel that now all the time.' She repeats this thought, for emphasis, 'I keep feeling that now I am meeting my mother again through my own experience as a mother.'

Simone recognises many more elements of her mother in her own behaviour.

I can talk to anyone, as could she. As a professional nurse she could talk to doctors or cleaning ladies. She taught me the skills of multi-discourse. I have never 'fitted in'. I can be in a liminal place all my life and be comfortable there: she taught me that. Her courage was enormous and it was the courage not to belong. That's how I think of her. She also taught me to argue and fight *for* things which were important, not *with* people. My 'good mother' said that conflicts are just badly expressed desires, so she taught me the language of desire.

Anne was one of the 'Daddy's girls' until her mother's death. 'I used to think I was more like my father than my mother, but now I recognise that I'm like her.' Like many of us, Anne had doubts as to her mother's feelings for her, resolved after her death. 'After she died, the people who knew her in Hartlepool told me how proud she was of what I had achieved.' Although when Anne spoke to me, eighteen months had gone by since the death of her mother, she admitted that she still had not come to terms with her loss; she was still in the raw, early stage of denial, guilt and anger. She had little time to follow the process of mourning for her mother, as her father died so soon afterwards. She had looked after him in her home when it became obvious that he was utterly heart-broken and unable to look after himself after his wife's death. The strength which she describes in her mother is visible in her, and in her life story, so we may have every confidence that she will find the strength to move on with her life now that she can begin to care for her own emotional needs.

Helen admits to a relationship with her mother that was not 'easy', not a good relationship, and this makes her adjustment to life after her mother's death not entirely comfortable. 'I wanted to be different from her when I was young but I now realise I am like her in lots of ways. I still feel uncomfortable with that. I don't like my intolerance, which I get from her. We were very close. I got over her death by my work.'

For Helen, work has always been a way of coping (and perhaps escaping?) from the more difficult emotions, as she recognises. Her feelings towards her mother are still a mixture of deep love, some discomfort both with herself and her relationship, and lingering guilt. Nevertheless she says of her mother 'When she died I realised that no one would ever accept me and love me totally the way she did. She was the rock for the whole of my life.'

To an outside observer, although supremely well balanced and confident in her present and professional persona, Helen is still wrestling with the last two of Worden's tasks of the mourning process, and with the need to reconcile her deep love for her mother with her need to dismiss her mother's influence over her life.

Jane has had more difficulty in moving forward, and completing the tasks of mourning. As time has gone by since her mother's death, she has begun to put aside the bad memories of the last years of her life and the rejecting unkindness of her will. She now recalls the strong, working mother who faced the snobbery of a small village which rejected her as an hotelier, and whom she admires. She also pays warm tribute to the mother who, in the midst of her own unbearable pain at the loss of her only son, still found a way to break the news to her daughter with a message of love and hope which has remained throughout the years.

Jane knows how much hope her mother placed in her, and how disappointed she was when her daughter's first job as a teacher seemed to be on a path which would not lead to the fame she wanted for her. The great successes of Jane's professional life came after her mother's death, and she now so wishes that her mother could have been still here to see them.

Jane's journey of finding has been helped by her mother's autobiography. She has read and re-read her mother's book in a search for the real mother, and in an attempt to understand her and herself. She says

> It is only when you become a mother yourself that you appreciate your mother's feelings. I am lucky to have the book my mother left; it is a record of her life and how she felt.
>
> I am like her in some ways, although I have always been more conscious of our differences. After she died, I felt bitterness at first because there appeared to have been rejection of me. One has to put those feelings behind and get on with things. I am fortunate in that I have my work, and in the years after her death a lot of exciting things started to happen for me. I found that you get more understanding in the end – more than I had when she was alive. I have got back to the real person she was, not the one she became at the end. Now I assume she is with a loving God, and she will be at peace.

Ana has come to an acceptance of her life without her mother, despite losing her at such an early age. Although she still feels sadness that her mother has not been there to share her children and her professional success, she nevertheless feels still close to her.

I am like her in many things. I share her interest in cooking and fashion, and high standards I certainly get from her. I have brought my children up with those high standards and with the faith she taught me.

I get strength from her; no one could get the better of her. I think we could both be flexible when necessary. In some ways there might seem a big gap between her life and mine. She lived in Africa and I have lived in England, and she had very little education while I am a qualified medical doctor. But she was a very successful businesswoman, and very ambitious for herself and for us children. I think she would be happy with me.

Poppy's visit to Sweden after her mother's death was very much a part of her journey of finding. She feels that she found not only much of the identity of her mother there, but also found some of her own, saying 'I had forgotten how Swedish I was!' Poppy too now recognises how much she is like her mother. As we have seen, she feels that she followed her mother's example in her relationship with her husband, even though she had been critical of her mother for being 'subservient' to her father. 'I feel I have been the same as my mother; I've followed my husband's career and never done anything in my own right.'

Poppy is too self-aware to claim that all the tasks of mourning have been completed, more than four years after her mother's death. 'I've never sorted out her stuff, so perhaps I haven't really let her go. Her bedroom is still full of her things.' Poppy is, however, a good example of a daughter who has no need to seek for any further or final 'letting go'. She has undoubtedly moved on happily with her own life without her mother, secure in the knowledge that she was loved, and 'feeling great' that her relationship with her mother was 'brilliant'. She feels all that needed to be said was said, and if now the 'place' to which her mother has been assigned is one still close to her, in the room along the hall, then most psychologists today would say that is a happy and healthy outcome.

Chapter Ten
Finding the Answers

When a mother dies, her daughter finds herself facing some of the most difficult and important questions of her life. The death of a parent, father or mother, for sons and daughters brings us face to face with our own mortality; our relationships with the next generation of our own children and our siblings' children; an awareness of the totality of our lives to that point; and the nature of love and loss. It is often our first experience of the death of anyone so close to us that we have experienced, and we find ourselves wrestling with the nature and meaning of death, which can only be found in our belief about the nature and meaning of life.

For all of us as daughters, our mother's death also leads us to face up as never before to questions about what it is to be a woman, and especially what it means to be a mother. Is the model of female identity the one which our mothers' generation accepted, or is it some new model which we and our daughters have to create? What is mother love? And what remains of it after death?

In the stories of ten articulate women whose memories of their mothers and their dying and loss we have shared, as well as in the published literature we have examined, it also becomes apparent that these and other questions become newly urgent in the months and years after we lose our mothers. Mothers give an identity to their daughters that is closer, more complex and more direct than in any other relationship. A boy is close in love and understanding to his mother throughout life; but it is to his father he

143

must turn for a model of male identity as he grows up. Daughters and fathers share a love and closeness throughout their lives. But a baby girl is a woman born of a woman. The closeness they share in the early years of life is also a passing on of female identity; of what it means to be a woman. The bond is unbreakable, and the relationship is unique. When it is broken by death, new questions about ourselves and who we are may arise.

As I listened to the words of the women I interviewed, and as I read some of the moving literature and autobiography which has been written about the experience of daughters at the loss of their mother, I became determined to see what the social scientists and philosophers had to say to throw light on these huge questions they were asking. What I found was an amazing world of research and analysis which, although not always providing answers, nevertheless opens up paths of understanding through which every individual can travel to find her own answers.

One of the first questions which occurs to many as they experience the intensity of shock and grief in bereavement is: what is it about the death of our mother that makes her loss so devastating, to sons and daughters alike? To answer this, we can look at the whole theme of attachment and loss, which anthropologists and psychologists have studied over many decades in relation to infant attachment to the mother figure.

Sarah Hrdy devotes considerable time to this phenomenon in her book *Mother Nature*. She describes the work done by the psychologist John Bowlby with a Cambridge ethologist Robert Hinde. Their collaboration gave us understanding of the way in which the young of many species develop, from birth, a life-sustaining and fierce attachment to their mother figure. At the time they began their research, in the 1950s, it was commonly assumed that this attachment was related to the infant's need for food, which the mother, and in most species only she, could provide.

Hinde had, however, been fascinated by the now famous experiments conducted at the University of Wisconsin by Professor Harry Harlow. Looking at the species from which our ancient ancestors had themselves evolved, Harlow had sought to find whether it was in fact the need for food – 'cupboard love' – which inspired the attachment of a child to its mother. He demonstrated that baby monkeys, removed from their own mothers and given a choice of a doll-mother made of soft cuddly material but offering no milk or one made from uncomfortable wire but with a milk bottle, would spend the minimum time with the uncomfortable 'milk mother', enough to satisfy their hunger, but would then rush back to the comfort of the soft, secure mother doll. In frightening or strange situations, it was the soft cuddly mother to whom the baby monkeys clung for comfort. This seemed to imply that what made a baby attach so strongly was not the satisfaction of its bodily hunger, but rather the satisfaction of a much more powerful hunger: the need for comfort and a sense of security.

In recounting these results, Hrdy comments that whatever it is that human babies exhibit in their attachment to their mothers, their emotions have their origins in time measured in millions of years. The need for mother-comfort is so strong, so built into our nature by generations of evolution, that those who seek to deny it must pay a vast emotional cost. While this attachment is true for all babies, male and female, how much stronger it must be for the females who retain their mother's gender identity for life. In almost all mammal species, it is daughters who remain near their mothers as adults.

If the attachment is so powerful, what, then does separation mean? Bowlby had already been studying the effect which separation from the mother had on human babies, and now set out with Hinde to see what effect separation from the mother-figure would have on the primate babies with which Hinde had been working. Hinde had noted that virtually all primate babies are in constant tactile contact with their mothers throughout their early lives. In his Cambridge experiments he had found that rhesus monkeys deprived of this contact exhibit a series of stages of emotion. First they protest, loudly and with cries which rend the hearts of their human keepers; next they fall into despair, often huddling silently in isolation and beyond the comfort of other monkeys or keepers; lastly, they become detached, in human terms we would say hardened. In this stage they reorganise their lives without the mother and look no longer to others for security.

It is not, I think, too fanciful to observe that these stages show some striking similarities to the stages of human bereavement. The attached baby goes through the stages of actively searching for the mother, by crying and calling; and then through the stage of realising and accepting that she is gone, so falling into despair; and finally reorganising her or his life to continue without the mother's presence.

Later experiments showed that such experiences of separation create lasting changes in the behaviour of the monkeys. Even years later, they were more timid, less inclined to be creative or to explore innovative solutions to challenges, than their contemporaries who had enjoyed continuous mother contact.

When these experiments were repeated with human babies, observing their reactions in a strange situation, very similar results were found. Interestingly, though, the researchers noted different reactions to the absence and subsequent return of the mother, depending on the relationship that already existed between them. Two-year-old toddlers behaved in much the same way as all primates, showing anxiety when the mother left, and jumping up, running to her and holding tight to her when she returned. The human toddlers, however, varied in the intensity of this response in direct proportion to the security they had already experienced in their relationship with their mother. The most secure seemed less anxious when she disappeared, and were less inclined to cling tightly when she reappeared, sometimes simply looking up and smiling with pleasure at her return. Those who had less satisfactory relationships of trust, however, clung the more desperately and tightly to the mother on her return, while those with the least secure relationship of all seemed wary and uncomfortable even in her presence and were preoccupied by their mother both before and after her return, failing to be comforted by her presence when she returned.

Again, there are lessons from these experiments which help us to understand the different reactions to the final earthly separation of mother and child. Daughters whose relationship with their mothers has been less than happy often find her death most difficult to bear. The searching for who she was, and what she and we meant to each other can be a very long and difficult road. One of the stark illustrations of this is to be found in the overwhelming need to search for their mother which is seen even, and perhaps most strongly, in those daughters with a less than happy relationship with their mother. Margaret Drabble's *Peppered Moth* is one extreme example; Anne Robinson's *Confessions of an Unfit Mother* is another, as are Vivian Gornick's *Fierce Attachments*, Genie Zeiger's *How I Find Her* and Paula Fox's *Borrowed Finery*.

Amongst the ten women of this book, this more painful kind of search is also clearly seen in the stories of Helen, Peggy, Anne, and Jane. None of them had wholly smooth relationships with their mother, even though all recognise the love which was there. In every case, they now acknowledge how much of their mother is in them; how much they have learned about who she was since her death, and how much they understand about themselves since finding more of their mother.

It was moving to me to hear the eagerness with which every woman wanted to praise her mother. Each emphasised her mother's beauty, attractiveness, intelligence and skill, even though some admitted they had not thought about or valued these qualities in their mother during her lifetime. It was also moving to hear them recall how their mother had always wanted 'the best' for them in every way. Even Helen, who complains that her mother never seemed impressed by her achievements nor acknowledged them to her, is anxious to record that her relatives told her that her mother had 'idolised' her, boasting to them about her clever and successful daughter.

The other women too have engaged in the search for their mother, in memories and in mementoes. Ana had so little time with the mother she lost at eighteen, but relives in present-day vivid detail her mother's character, appearance and achievements, recognising the debt she owes her in her own life and her own identity. A. feels that her life is far removed from that of her mother, yet acknowledges that much of her core identity comes from the woman whose saris she wore with such pride for many years after her death.

Judith, another 'Daddy's girl' in her childhood, finds herself now reflecting on the similarity between herself and her mother, for example, in the role of a mother-in-law. Simone and Jinny, both in different ways such close and devoted daughters, are still engaged in finding more about their mothers, in understanding behaviour they took for granted as girls growing up, years after their mothers have died.

These are stories, stories of individuals which nevertheless form a pattern, but they ask and can only in part answer the second great question: 'What is female identity?' 'What is a woman?'

For feminist psychologists and philosophers the answer has always been a source of debate and controversy. On the one hand, there was understandable and justifiable anger on the part of the earliest feminists at the 'subjugation' of women in society. The female character, they argued, had been shaped by the male dominant culture to be compliant, caring and subservient. Their belief was that women needed to recognise these characteristics as self-destructive, designed to keep them in the lowly place in society where for some generations they had remained. To break free, women needed to learn the successful male characteristics which they characterised as aggressive, assertive, ambitious and self-confident: the qualities needed for leadership in the world as it then was.

Conversely, others argued that what was really 'wrong' was a society which only rewarded those male characteristics, and which undervalued the strengths which women could bring to bear. Women, they argued, whether by nature or nurture (a separate debate) had learned to negotiate not dominate, to show care for the feelings of others, and to nurture and reward others. These skills, they asserted, would provide the balance to male skills in business, the professions and public life, and in so doing would create a better, kinder world.

The latter arguments received support from an unexpected source. After the recession of the early 1980s, a team of researchers, Tom Peters and Nancy Austin, published a revolutionary book, *A Passion for Excellence*, about the leadership style which had proved successful in keeping business afloat during the recession and beyond. They demonstrated, with hundreds of examples, that the old 'assertive' dominant leader was now no longer appropriate. The style that was succeeding in the mid 1980s was one where recognition of one's employees and one's customers as important and valued human beings was paramount; where 'walking about' was more valuable that sitting behind a large and impressive desk all day; and where creativity and innovation were the secret of corporate success.

Feminists were quick to recognise and publicise that these were characteristics which women had mastered to perfection over many generations. The 'softer' and more human face of management style was one where women could claim their place alongside men as equals or better. The succeeding decades, while still retaining the gender imbalance of the boardroom heavily in favour of men, have nevertheless seen women rising to the very top of some of our largest corporations, and proving their talent and skill in ways of which their mother's generation could hardly have dreamed. In other words, those who believed that it was social mores which needed to change, not women, were more right than those who wanted women to become more like men.

Although events proved those who wanted society to change were 'more right' than those who wanted to change women, nevertheless they were not wholly right. It was essential for women of my generation, born in the middle of the last century, to make changes in themselves if they were to be able to succeed in the still male-orientated world of their adult lives. This meant that we needed to become different from most of our mothers in various key ways. At the time when Betty Friedan was writing her ground-breaking feminist book, *The Feminine Mystique*, in the mid 1960s, it is amazing to reflect that more than half of the twenty year olds in the United States were already married. This was 'our generation' to which the women in this book, and many of the authors quoted belong. Although we had been able to benefit from the educational opportunities which had been so hard won by the pioneers of our mothers' generation, it seems that most of us still regarded early marriage and families as the most desirable end for our adult lives.

Friedan's genius, and the reason for her book's astonishing success, was that she spoke to that generation, making us look at ourselves and the way we had chosen to live our lives with new eyes. She addressed the nagging questions about women's identity when she spoke of what it meant to be a mother. She said in plain English that most of us were neither happy nor fulfilled by the life we were living, centred on housework and children, and pointed out how much advertising revenue had been poured into keeping us as happy housewife consumers of the many goods which western manufacturers were pouring on to the market in the boom years of the 1960s. She also made us aware that we were not necessarily good wives and mothers if we were frustrated in our own lives. Many women of that time, unable to achieve themselves, were obliged to nag and push their husbands and children to achieve on their behalf, and to 'take out' their frustration on the family.

Sarah Hrdy would concur with Friedan's conclusions in this aspect at least. Hrdy's observation of primates throws new light on what it means to be a woman and a mother. In earlier studies of animal behaviour, undertaken mainly by men, little attention had been paid to the perspective of the female of the species. Only in the second half of the twentieth century was this bias slowly corrected by observers such as Hrdy and Jeanne Altman. Hrdy quotes Altmann's work with particular admiration. She was determined to observe mother baboons in their natural habitat, not in the isolated cages which had so often been used to discover the 'nature' of mothering in primates. Animal mothers, she pointed out, behave very unnaturally when shut up in cages with only their young for company, and with no need either to search and compete for food or to protect themselves and their young from the predators of their natural habitat. In retrospect, it is amazing that male anthropologists had believed that any reliable understanding of maternal primate behaviour could be gained from such observations.

Altmann, observing animals in the wild with scientific and measured care, found that in normal surroundings every mother baboon was a 'dual-career' mother, obliged by necessity to spend the greater part of every day searching for food and avoiding predators while also caring for her infant. The mother is a part of the life of the totality of the baboon troop and gives, Altmann found, perhaps seventy per cent of her time to 'work' which is shared by the male and female members alike.

The importance of Hrdy's own work in observing maternal behaviour in primates is her understanding of the harsh choices they have to make if they and their offspring are to survive. The luxury of large families is not given to animals who must work ceaselessly just to survive. We know that amongst human beings, even wealthy western women will limit their family to two or three children in order to have sufficient funds to provide an expensive education for their children and rich dowry for their daughters. Primate mothers may choose to sacrifice or even kill some of their offspring if they produce too many to support, and almost all will spread their breeding over their reproductive lives in order both to preserve their own strength and their offspring's chances of survival.

Hrdy draws a parallel between this ruthless animal behaviour and the topic from which in the West most of us recoil in horror today: infanticide. In our society infanticide is, rightly, a most abhorrent crime; but in many societies of the developing world, it is as much a choice for survival of mother and other children as it was for the primates which Hrdy observed. We have all heard with horror stories of girl babies being put out to die from exposure in poor societies where girls are considered of low value in their labour, and expensive in their dowry, and this practice is still found in some parts of the world.

My sister-in-law told me her personal experience of her distress when, living as a young Englishwoman in Nigeria, she took pity on the youngest child of one of her poor neighbours in the servants' compound. Noting how weak and poorly dressed the girl seemed to be in comparison with her siblings, my sister-in-law gave her food and warm clothes on several occasions. She noticed, however, that the clothes were always passed quickly to the other children, and any food which remained was similarly snatched away. Eventually, and with tears, the little girl's mother told her that this was the child who had to be allowed to die because the family could not afford to keep her, and her husband had decreed that she was not to be fed or sheltered. The mother had accepted the force of the decision, even though her instinct was that of any mother unwilling to lose her child.

Hrdy also tackles the related and uncomfortable topic of abandoned children. In the eighteenth century, many foundling homes were provided by the church and sometimes by local communities to allow mothers who were unable to provide for their newborn babies a way to abandon their children with the hope – sadly not often realised – that they would be cared for and enabled to survive. The explicit intention of these homes was to prevent the

151

death of the child, either from neglect and starvation or from infanticide. People in Europe were concerned at the large numbers of abandoned infants which were daily found in gutters, rivers and by the roadside, and so the well-intentioned movement to provide foundling homes as an alternative was begun.

Tragically, the provision only served to bring out into the open the enormity of the problem. In times when birth control was almost unknown and poverty was rife, thousands of unwanted babies were dumped on the doorsteps of the foundling homes each year. The homes, under-equipped and often staffed by people who knew little of even the most basic rules of hygiene or child care, became focal points for lethal diseases with mortality rates in some cases of over ninety per cent.

These shocking stories, from which we turn away our minds and attention even today, demonstrate, as Hrdy argues, that the behaviour of human mothers is, in difficult circumstances, as ruthless in the pursuit of survival for themselves and their existing children as is the behaviour of much of the animal kingdom she observed. The sentimentality of visions of motherhood, in which every mother achieves her highest heaven in caring for her every baby, belong mainly to the fantasies of the advertising industry, and sit oddly with the huge and growing number of abortions carried out each year throughout the developed world. The luxury of choice in motherhood belongs to societies affluent and educated enough that families can be limited to the small number of children their parents can afford to keep in comfort with every expectation of their survival.

The nature of motherhood, then, includes some very nonsentimental elements. Fierce in their defence of their young, mothers can also, in extreme circumstances, be forced into decisions which may result in the death of the weaker and newer offspring. Trade-offs have to be made by mothers in the animal kingdom, and in the poorest of the human kingdom such painful trade-offs are sometimes also forced on human mothers.

Does this make of the vision of the tender and loving mother a myth? Quite the contrary, Hrdy says. The supreme motivation for a mother is firstly her own survival in order to care for her young, and then the welfare of her healthy young, who will ensure the continuance of her family. Mothers of all species are, therefore, programmed by their evolutionary inheritance to be deeply, passionately devoted and caring mothers to their young. The conflict between nurturing and tender with ruthless and competitive is not a real one, since both are the successful mother's means of ensuring the welfare of her loved infant. Her ambition is the good and praiseworthy ambition to secure 'the best' for her young, by her efforts and skills.

This has the strongest resonance with all we have heard from daughters talking about their mothers. The determination and effort put into the survival of the family, as well as the pursuit of 'the best' for their daughters are not so far removed from the motivation and behaviour of the primates in their natural habitat. In the behaviour of the splendid women we have met in this book through their daughters, there has been ample evidence of how mothers pass on the gift of adaptive survival.

Translated into the demands of the twenty-first century, these daughters learned from their mothers how to use their unique gifts in a variety of challenging circumstances. They can adapt to hugely differing social groups as well as to the use and mastery of new technologies. They have emerged intact from childhoods marred by war and its aftermath, and welcomed, indeed in some cases initiated, changes in society unparalleled in former generations. All but one of them have become loving and fiercely defending mothers themselves, passing on to their sons and daughters a new and adapted version of the skills of survival in a world yet to come. It is difficult, listening to them, not to echo silently the often-repeated, 'If only my mother could have been there to see how well I have done'. I know with perfect assurance that each of their mothers would indeed be proud of what her daughter has done. I suspect each died confident in the future for her much-loved girl-child; after all, they would say, she is my daughter and I loved her well.

The insights which the evolutionary anthropologists and psychologists have contributed to our understanding of human behaviour are immensely rewarding. The fundamental unity of the whole human race in patterns of family, friendship, collaborative work with one's own community and even morality are explained by the process of evolution which has filtered out behaviours that are negative to survival. Over many generations of evolution, the young of mothers who failed to love, nurture and protect their young could not survive to maturity, and so the genes responsible for such failure were slowly eliminated from the pool. The fierce love of a mother for her children, like their fierce need of mothering, is as much a part of the evolved nature of mothering as the air we breathe.

Does this evolutionary insight mean that there is no choice? Is evolution only determinism by another name? Not so, says the evolutionary psychologist Robert Wright. Within the exciting unity of one universal human nature, natural selection has also ensured that the characteristic of *adaptability* has enabled human beings to react appropriately to their differing environments. The nature-nurture debate is, then, another of the either-or debates which can be easily resolved by the answer 'both'. Human beings share a common human nature, which also allows them to react to their particular family and society in ways which ensure their survival. Mothers in one society and generation will behave in ways which seem very different from those in another. Nurture, then, explains those visible differences, but the basic and enduring relationship of mother and child derives from the evolved nature of what it is to be a successful mother in any environment.

In the light of these insights, it is no longer surprising to find that the young women of the generation now in their twenties have absorbed both the career expectations of their mothers and the traditional role expectations of their grandmothers. Distanced by one generation from the first feminists, they seem to have adapted to be more comfortable and confident in all that a dual-career mother of the primate species instinctively knew was right for the female and her young to survive.

This book has been about daughters and their mothers, but in a powerful way it has been about love. I make no apology for using that word, since it has occurred over and over in the testimony of these daughter-witnesses. Each has spoken of her love for her mother, as well as of her mother's love for her. Many described their mother's love as the rock on which they had built their lives; others spoke of the certainty that when they lost their mother, they knew that no one would ever accept and love them again in the total and unquestioning way that their mothers had done. In so speaking, they have answered the question of what is mother love for themselves. A mother's love for her child, like the attachment of child to mother, has its origins, as we have seen, in our evolutionary ancestry of many millions of years, and to deny it is a painful and ultimately destructive act. Mothers who reject their daughters, and daughters who try to reject their mothers, pay a terrifyingly high emotional price. The forces of those millions of years of evolutionary heritage are against them.

For women whose experience of mothering has been less happy, rejection may seem a logical decision. But Anita Diament says, through the words of Dinah in *The Red Tent*, that the more a daughter knows the details of her mother's life, the stronger she will be. She adds that the daughter must face all that her mother was, without 'flinching or whining'. Many women have found this to be true. In facing and forgiving the failures in our mother's life as well as in her mothering, we can learn to face and forgive ourselves, and those things in our personality and behaviour which we have from her.

Women who have suffered negative experiences of mothering often worry that they will inevitably repeat these negative behaviours in their own adult life. For them, the burden of the mother-daughter chain can be heavy indeed. The psychoanalyst Michael Rutter argues, however, that repetition and continuity of 'bad' behaviour is not inevitable. Daughters are not doomed to repeat the mistakes and deficiencies of their childhood experience, nor to incorporate those parts of their mother they most fear and reject. He found that two factors are critical in breaking the negative cycle. Daughters who are able to express their justifiable anger towards their mother when they are children and who can then find forgiveness for her in their adult lives are freed from the cycle. Secondly, a daughter who has an alternative and supportive adult to turn to, who helps her to develop and preserve her self-esteem in childhood and adolescence, escapes the permanent damage of poor mothering and so breaks free of the need to repeat such behaviour in her own adult life.

What some women have found also is that the ability to forgive and understand comes only after the death of their mother. With that forgiveness and understanding comes for them the freedom to cast off the negative inheritance and accept the wealth of positive inheritance which is their mother's gift.

The last great questions are about the nature of death. This book is also about death, and about the questions and answers which daughters ask and find through the death of their mother. The Song of Solomon tells us 'love is as strong as death' and our stories have given form and beauty to that message. A daughter's love for her mother breathes through each of the women's accounts of her memories of childhood, the relationship in adult life, the caring in dying and the pain of parting. Triumphantly, though, the stories also tell of each daughter's searching for knowledge and understanding of her mother, and how death and loss is the beginning of a new way of relating to her mother, and a new way of understanding the meaning of what it is to be a woman. The women's strong sense of the presence of their mother, and their recognition of how much of her is in them, is a liberating and joyous insight into the relationship of mother to daughter, of one generation of women to another.

All major religions teach that death is only the beginning of another, eternal life; humanists and others believe that immortality resides in the memories of those who loved us. I heard no word from any of the ten women I interviewed nor did I find in literature anyone who denied that the dead are still present for the living, in whatever way that presence is described.

The death of a most-loved mother brings into focus the meaning of life, and the basis of our beliefs, religious or other. For many of the women who spoke to me, religion was a central part of both their own and their mother's life, and so important to them in the way they thought about the meaning of death and life. In his book *The Meanings of Death*, John Bowker explores the way in which humanism and the major religions interpret death. It is his immensely comforting and life-enhancing conclusion that there cannot be life on any other terms than those of death. Both science and religion know this to be true, and so in our hearts we know that death and birth are twin sisters of each other.

Writing as a Christian theologian in his most recent book *The Church that Could Be*, David Edwards puts the Christian faith in the love of God most clearly: 'The God that loves persons can love them to, and beyond, death'. It is this faith which sustains not only Christians but members of many other religions, in thinking about the future of the loved one and indeed in contemplating the certainty of their own death. 'She is with a loving God,' said Jane of her mother, and even so do many daughters comfort themselves as they mourn.

Bowker illustrates vividly the way in which the major religions have developed a coherent set of beliefs over many centuries. This coherence is not accidental; it reflects the cumulative wisdom and experience of millions of human beings across time and distance, across differing cultures and social groupings. Over hundreds of generations, men and women have interpreted their common experience in the light of the science known to them in their time and place. This common experience has shaped the tenets of their religious belief, just as it has determined the rituals of death and dying, which we saw in Chapter Seven.

Bowker argues that belief in a life after death is a recognition by all human observers that it is only from death that life can come; in nature it is necessary for one form of life to die if another is to be born. The value and importance of death for the living is therefore recognised by scientific observation just as it is felt most personally by the bereaved as they search for meaning in their grief. In sacrifice, he says, both science and religion meet and reinforce each other.

Although sacrifice is not an easy concept for the twenty-first century, it is nevertheless important that we understand its origin. Sacrifice was an important part of the early Jewish and Muslim religions, and seems also to have been an essential element in many other ancient religions too. The concept of Christ as the 'one perfect sacrifice' is also at the heart of Christianity. The origins of what to us may seem a distasteful and pseudomagical custom, though, lie in the recognition by our ancestors of that essential truth that death is necessary for life to continue.

As a humanist and scientific observer, Bowker invites us, if we doubt the evidence of nature, to look at our own hand and reflect on what scientists now know about the origins of living cells. Some millions of years ago most of the atoms which make up that hand were part of some distant star twinkling across light years towards our planet. Our hand, like every part of our body, is composed of carbon from a long-dead star; it lives only because a star died. Further, though, evolution itself requires death. The changes needed for human development and for survival as conditions change require the passage of many generations. Unless one generation gives way to the next, the very development of our species would come to a halt. Life requires death, as the universe requires death. But in dying, we create life; we make life possible.

The humanist offers this dynamic picture of death, and gives it meaning on the global scale, while the believer understands this but also sees that God cares for each individual creature. The believer of almost any religion feels confident that after the death of one human being, some of their essential personality remains in God's hands, just as some part of them remains in the memories and love of those close to them.

For the Christian, the resurrection of Jesus Christ is the ultimate truth. Life can come from death, and the resurrection of Jesus Christ gives to all human beings the possibility that in His rising from the dead we can all be 'made alive', that is, that for us too, life will spring from death. For the followers of many other great religions the same confidence is found. Although we may falter in our imagining of what it means to have life after death or what that life may be, we rest assured in our faith that the person we love is in the care of the God who made her and that in some way beyond our understanding, the life we value and cherish is not lost.

What can we learn from the experts whose writings I have tried to outline? Positive messages abound, to give comfort to the bereaved in our grief and guilt. Many of the negative and unhappy aspects of bereavement prove, on examination, to be the gateway to positive and life-affirming growth and understanding. The loss and pain of death are, in all beliefs, only the beginning of new life and a new freedom in love. Guilt about not being present at the moment of our mother's death proves to be as misplaced as the guilt of not giving up a career to care for her. I hope the evidence that both of these decisions and events may be her choice as much as ours will be a comfort to women who carry this heavy burden.

The ambivalence of the female condition and the contradictions in the nature of motherhood can be seen to be an unhappy development of the past two centuries or so. The real nature of motherhood – and of women – stems from much older and more certain evolutionary success. Furthermore, we are not, it seems, doomed to repeat our mother's failures, nor to be slaves to her more obsolete habits. We do not need to choose whether we are like our mother or like our father; both contribute to who we are as women and how confidently we face the world. The dichotomies of either-or in career and motherhood, even faith or agnosticism are, in the literal sense, man-made and ephemeral. Even the age-old dichotomy of nature or nurture as the determinant of who and how we are proves capable of resolution when we understand that evolution has both given us a common human nature and also the ability to adapt that nature to changing environment and circumstance.

In my research for this book, and in talking to those ten women, the messages which have come through to me are profoundly inspiring messages of hope. The answers to our questions about the nature of mothering, about female identity and the meaning of death and life come into a sharp focus in the bonds of mother-to-daughter love and shared identity, across more generations than we can imagine. We are the current bearers of the evolutionary successes of thousands of our female ancestors, and their wisdom and cumulative practice as women and as mothers as well as daughters of their mothers is the priceless inheritance we carry.

All women throughout history and throughout the world share one thing in common; we are all the daughters of mothers. Small wonder that the common characteristics we share are greater than the differences which seem to separate us. The inheritance we bring to the market place of our respective societies has an unmatched richness to contribute to boardroom decision making, national and local government, trades union or parliamentary debate and academic endeavour, just as it has to family life and community activity. The struggle to balance work and life stems from a male-imposed form of society which would be meaning-less to our primate ancestors, and should be meaningless to us today if our ways of conducting public and business affairs were not so unwisely designed by and for the males of a previous generation.

One of the great traditions we inherit is that of quiet and bloodless revolution. Our great-great-grandmothers, like the mothers we have seen in these stories, knew how to adapt social custom and initiate enormous change in the way things were done simply by using their collective, powerful influence to bring change about when it was needed. I believe that quiet revolutionary tradition is being followed today, in the battle for better living conditions for women in the developing world as much as in the battle for work-life balance in the West. As participants in that revolution, we draw not only on the strengths of our own generation of women around the world, but on the unimaginable strength of women from all the generations past. Recognising and welcoming them as part of our identity gives to each of us and to all women collectively a power and joy beyond imagination.

Hope Edelman puts it well, when she talks of the power of the generations. She says that her great-grandmother, her grandmother and so on, down to her child and the grandchild of the future are like the Russian dolls which unpack slowly one inside the other. All the past generations are there inside us, just as we are in our children and grandchildren. As she watches her own little daughter playing the piano, using the same gestures and expressions as her long-dead grandmother and great-grandmother did before her, Hope realises how much of them is still alive in her daughter. Saluting her female ancestors, she says of her daughter 'She is their song'.

The songs of the women in ancient times carried the wisdom of their tribes from one generation to the next. In recent generations – but a fleeting moment in the millions of years of evolution – the distinctive songs of women have perhaps not been heard as clearly as they once were, and as they should be if the world is to use all its human resources to build a strong and fairer future. The generation of women represented in these stories have with their mothers' strength and blessing, begun to sing more confidently and in tune with their female contemporaries across national, racial and cultural boundaries. Our daughters and granddaughters will, I believe, again sing fearlessly the song of all our splendid female ancestors. When they do, oh yes then, the music of unending generations of mothers and daughters will shake the world with love.

References

ADELMAN, HOPE (1999). *Mother of My Mother*. New York: Dell Publishing.

ALTMANN, JEANNE (1989). *Baboon Mothers and Infants*, Cambridge, Mass.: Harvard University Press.

APTER, T. E. (1990). *Altered Loves*. New York: St Martin's Press.

ARMSTRONG, CAMPBELL (2000). *All That Really Matters*, London: Little Brown & Co.

ARNOT, MADELAINE, WEINER, GABY and DAVID, MIRIAM (1999). *Closing the Gender Gap*, Cambridge: Polity Press.

BARFORD, WANDA (1999). *A Moon at the Door*, Hexham: Flambard Press.

BOWKER, JOHN (1991). *The Meanings of Death*. Cambridge University Press.

BOWLBY, JOHN (1961). Processes of Mourning. *International Journal of Psychoanalysis*, 44.

— (1991). 'Ethological Light on Psychoanalytical Problems'. In *The Development and Integration of Behaviour* ed. Bateson, Patrick: Cambridge: Cambridge University Press.

— (1969). *Attachment and Loss*. vol. 1. Harmondsworth: Penguin Books.

COWARD, ROSALIND (1999). *Sacred Cows*, London: Harper Collins.

DIAMENT, ANITA (1997). *The Red Tent*, New York: St Martin's Press.

DRABBLE, MARGARET (2000). *The Peppered Moth*. London: Viking.

EDWARDS, DAVID (2002). *The Church that Could Be*. London: SPCK.

FORSTER, MARGARET (2000). *The Memory Box*. London: Penguin.

FOX, PAULA (2002). *Borrowed Finery*. London: Flamingo.

FRANCIS, DORIS, KELLAHER, LEONIE and NEOPHYTOU GEORGINA (2000). 'Sustaining Cemeteries: The User Perspective' In *Mortality*, vol. 5.

FRIDAY, NANCY (1979). *My Mother My Self.* London: Fontana.

FRIEDAN, BETTY (1963). *The Feminine Mystique.* Harmondsworth: Penguin.

FRENCH, MARILYN (1977). *The Women's Room.* New York: W.W. Norton.

GAVRON, HANNAH (1966). *The Captive Wife,* London: Routledge & Kegan Paul.

GORNICK, VIVIAN (1987). *Fierce Attachments.* New York: Simon & Schuster.

GREER, GERMAINE (1970). *The Female Eunuch.* London: Granada Publishing.

GRIMSHAW, JEAN (1986). *Philosophy and Feminist Thinking.* Minneapolis: University of Minnesota Press.

HAKIM, K. (1993). 'The Myth of Rising Female Employment' In *Work Employment and Society* no. 7.

HERTZ, ROBERT (1960). *Death and the Right Hand,* trans. Rodney and Claudia Needham. London: Cohen & West.

HEWLETT, SYLVIA ANN (2002). *Baby Hunger.* London: Atlantic Books.

HRDY, SARAH BLAFFER (2000). *Mother Nature.* London: Vintage.

HUNTINGDON, R. and METCALF, P. (1979). *Celebrations of Death: The Anthropology of Mortuary Ritual.* Cambridge: Cambridge University Press.

IRONSIDE, VIRGINIA (1996). *You'll Get Over It.* London: Hamish Hamilton.

KUBLER-ROSS, ELIZABETH (1970). *On Death and Dying.* London: Tavistock Publications.

LINDEMANN, E. (1944). 'The Symptomatology and Management of Acute Grief,' *American Journal of Psychiatry.*

MASON, JERRY, ed. (1979). *The Family of Woman.* New York: Grosset & Dunlap.

MILLETT, KATE (2001). *Mother Millett.* London: Verso.

ORBACH, SUSIE (1978). *Fat is a Feminist Issue.* New York & London: Paddington Press.

PETERS, THOMAS J. and AUSTIN, NANCY K. (1985). *A Passion for Excellence.* New York: Random House.

REES, DEWI (1997). *Death and Bereavement.* London: Whurr Publishers Ltd.

WORDEN, J. W. (1991). *Grief Counselling and Grief Therapy.* London: Routledge.

References

WRIGHT, ROBERT (1994). *The Moral Animal*. New York: Random House.

ZEIGER, GENIE (2001). *How I Find Her*. Santa Fe: Sherman Asher Publishing.